Haunted Pennsylvania

Ghosts and Strange Phenomena
of the Keystone State

Mark Nesbitt and Patty A. Wilson
Illustrations by Heather Adel Wiggins

STACKPOLE
BOOKS

Published by
STACKPOLE BOOKS
5067 Ritter Road
Mechanicsburg, PA 17055
www.stackpolebooks.com

Printed in the United States of America

10 9 8 7 6 5 4

FIRST EDITION

Design by Beth Oberholtzer
Cover design by Caroline Stover

Library of Congress Cataloging-in-Publication Data

Nesbitt, Mark.
Haunted Pennsylvania : ghosts and strange phenomena of the Keystone State / Mark Nesbitt and Patty A. Wilson ; illustrations by Heather Adel Wiggins. — 1st ed.
p. cm.
Includes bibliographical references.
ISBN-13: 978-0-8117-3298-7 (pbk.)
ISBN-10: 0-8117-3298-3 (pbk.)
1. Ghosts—Pennsylvania. 2. Monsters—Pennsylvania. 3. Haunted places—Pennsylvania. I. Wilson, Patty A. II. Title.
BF1472.U6N486 2006
133.109748—dc22 2006010129

Contents

Introduction

All human endeavor, all the strife of living, the pains and temptations, the suffering to achieve, the enduring and prevailing, all that we seek and all that we abhor, boils down to one question: Is this all there is?

We turn to religion to assure us—some 6 billion of us presently and countless billions from ages past—that there is an existence after this one; that once we shuffle off this mortal coil, there is something that abides, that death represents an opening—and not a closing—door.

And while we are not sure exactly what awaits us personally—eternal paradise or eternal damnation—we feel comforted in the hope that *something* awaits us, not just the moist, wormy grave.

Protohumans buried their dead some seventy thousand years ago with food, tools, clothes, and vehicles to assist in their passage through the next life. One must wonder how this unusual custom got started: Were our predecessors visited by one recently deceased who informed them of the needs of the dead?

Of course, it *is* much more than just what happens to the corporeal body. It is personal. Though Christians believe in actual, physical, bodily resurrection, to many the details of what happens to us eventually, at "the end of the age," does not matter as much as what happens to us immediately, in that very moment after death. Because it is at that moment when we will know for sure, one way or another, whether there is life after death.

Or, some say, maybe not. In spite of the fact that all major religions of the world assure us that our personalities, our souls, our essences survive death, somehow that is not enough. For some reason, we need more assurance.

And perhaps that is why we, as humans, are so fascinated with ghost stories.

It is not so much the fright factor as it is the assurance factor. Ghost stories give us proof positive that something of us goes on after our physical death. So in spite of what has been taught to us by our priests, ministers, and imams, we still refuse to believe in anything we cannot hear, see, or touch. Even if it is just a wispy, indistinct wraith, swirling through a neighborhood field, or the sound of footsteps creaking down the stairs where no one visible descends.

That is why, on those dark and stormy nights, in spite of the risk of having the living daylights scared out of us, we all still love a good ghost story.

Philadelphia Region

IT HAS BEEN SAID THAT PHILADELPHIA IS A SEPARATE STATE AND someone forgot to mention it to the mapmakers. Indeed, Philadelphia does seem like a world apart from the rest of Pennsylvania. It's one of the oldest cities in the nation and certainly was one of the most influential ones in the world during the 1700s. Here men like Ben Franklin shaped not only a nation, but a people. Here the nation was born.

The first settlers to arrive here lived in the caves along the waterways, but today Philadelphia has forgotten its more humble beginnings and is a world-class city whose residents are more cosmopolitan than those in most other parts of the state. Still, the past continues to play a big part.

The Many Spirits of the General Wayne Inn

The village of Merioneth, Pennsylvania, lies just outside Philadelphia. It was of importance in the Colonial period because it was conveniently placed for travelers westward. The General Wayne Inn was originally built in 1704 as an inn and tavern called the Wayside Inn. Robert Jones had purchased the land from Edward Rees, who in turn had bought it from William Penn but never used it.

The Wayside Inn grew popular with those traveling westward, and Jones ran a very successful inn and tavern for forty-two years. Upon Jones's death, the property was sold to Anthony Tunis, who changed the name of the establishment to the Ordinary Tunis. Tunis added a new concept that made his tavern and inn even more popular: He offered travelers a prix fixe meal, food that was already prepared and they could eat while the stagecoach drivers changed horses. The standard fare for travelers in a hurry was pork meat pies and grog (equal parts of water and rum). During this time, Tunis also allowed the building to be used as a mail stop. Benjamin Franklin was appointed by King George III of England as postmaster for the colonies, and he set up a post office at the Ordinary Tunis.

In May 1776, the Ordinary Tunis changed hands once more, when Abraham Streeper and his wife purchased the building. They changed the name to Streeper's Inn and continued to run it as a tavern and inn. Soon a call was put out for men to join the Colonial Army, and Abraham Streeper enlisted. His wife struggled to run the business herself.

Soon after her husband left, General "Mad Anthony" Wayne and the remainder of his men descended upon the inn, fresh from a terrible defeat at Brandywine. Wayne stayed there the first night, while his men camped out in the fields around the building. The next day, the Marquis de Lafayette and George Washington rode in to speak with Wayne and spent the night there as well.

The military left the following day, but soon a coach swept in with six members of the Continental Congress who were fleeing to York for fear that the British would take over Philadelphia and have them executed as traitors. Among them were James Smith, John Wilson, George Ross, and George Clymer (who would later be captured and hanged for treason by the British). The families of those men would soon follow them to the inn.

Mrs. Streeper had decidedly Colonial sympathies, and it soon became evident that Streeper's Inn was a good place for the Americans to spy. The place was frequented by British soldiers and Hessian (German) mercenaries who drank freely and sometimes talked too much. Chief among the spies was Captain Allen McLane, who gathered information as Mrs. Streeper supplied the enemy with liquor.

But Streeper's Inn soon was taken over by the British and Hessians, who commandeered the place for quarters. This made spying much more dangerous, and Colonial sympathizers could no longer travel freely in and out. Mrs. Streeper's life also could be in danger. Captain McLane liberated the building from the possession of the Hessians through the use of a trick and the liberal flow of alcohol, but the patriots held the building for only a short time before Philadelphia and the surrounding area fell into British hands again. The patriots were driven out, but rumors began to make the rounds that they had dug a tunnel into the basement of the building.

As the story goes, after a successful battle, a Hessian soldier was sent to the basement to fetch a cask of liquor. He never returned, and his body was not discovered. According to legend, the patriots were hiding in the tunnel and feared exposure, so they killed the young Hessian and buried his body in the tunnel. Perhaps this is how the very first ghost in the building was created.

In 1848, that old legend would be remembered after a most unlikely event. For fifty years or more, the local polling site for Lower Merion Township was at the inn, which had by now been renamed for General Wayne. According to the official report filed by the supervisor of the polling site, a female polling agent went to the basement to fetch a new box of ballots. There she encountered a young soldier wearing a green coat, who seemed startled or frightened before he faded away. The poll worker felt that the young man was scared and trying to hide. Hessian soldiers wore green jackets trimmed with yellow. Could it have been the ghost of the soldier who was killed there so long ago?

Over the years, more sightings of the Hessian soldier have been reported. In fact, more than one modern employee of the General Wayne Inn has insisted that he or she has seen the young man in green. They always say that he seems frightened and unsure and quickly fades away.

There are other possible explanations for the Hessian soldier. Mrs. Streeper pretended to be a British sympathizer, allowing the Hessians to bring their wounded to the inn and housing them there. It is believed that a sick Hessian was housed in the basement at one time. He supposedly died down there of his injuries while being tended by Mrs. Streeper. Some people even believe that Mrs.

Streeper murdered the young man and that's why he still haunts the building. That poor fellow may still be down there, sick and alone, afraid that patriot sympathizers will find him.

According to another story, at the end of the war, the Hessian soldiers who were left in America were abandoned by the British. Those men were terrified that they'd be found in uniform or recognized and executed by the patriots, so they took to hiding in spots where they had stayed while working for the British. Legend has it that a couple such Hessian soldiers sought refuge from the Americans in the basement of the inn. The men stayed there for some time during the winter, but one of them got ill and died of pneumonia. The poor fellow was too frightened to leave the cold, damp basement for better lodgings and medical help. Could he be the young Hessian who is still seen in the basement of the General Wayne Inn?

Other ghosts of Revolutionary War soldiers have also been seen in the building. In the early 1990s, a hostess said she had such an encounter. She was setting one of the dining areas up for dinner when she heard someone call her name. The person was insistent, so she paused to turn around, much annoyed at the intrusion. She was startled to see a man in a uniform that may have been a general standing on the steps near her. He seemed surprised that she heard and saw him and quickly faded away. The hostess described the man as having been very solid and real looking.

In the 1990s, a maître d' claimed to have been given quite a fright by a Hessian soldier. Some stories say that a Hessian soldier was ambushed in the building and killed by the patriots, who cut off his head and then disposed of the dead body. According to the maître d', he was walking by a cupboard in the kitchen one evening when he saw the head of a man materialize on a shelf. The man had a black mustache and was looking at him. The maître d' walked on past the head and out of the kitchen, when suddenly he stopped and began to shout, "I saw a head! I saw a head!" It was as if it took a second for him to register the gristly sight. Later, the maître d' insisted that the figure's black hair and mustache looked like those of Hessian soldiers from the Revolutionary period that he saw in paintings.

Yet another soldier is said to haunt the building, and his is a sad, romantic story. A young British officer was brought back to the

General Wayne Inn after he was wounded in battle. Despite the best efforts of the physician, the man died. During his last hours, he clutched constantly a little gold locket. After his death, the locket was removed from his hand and opened up. Inside was a fine miniature painting of a young woman who was presumed to be his fiancée. The locket was taken away, and the young soldier was buried. Over the years, several people have reported that a young British officer has appeared to them and demanded that they return his locket. When the astonished person does not respond to his plea, the soldier simply vanishes.

Another mysterious story was told by one of the former owners of the General Wayne Inn. During the 1970s and beyond, the building was owned by Barton Johnson. Each year at Christmas, the General Wayne Inn hosted a large Christmas gala. One year, at the end of the night, as the guests thanked him for his lovely party, several commented that they had enjoyed his little historical touch. Johnson was puzzled because he did not know what they were referring to. The guests explained that they had been much impressed with the young man he had hired to pass among the guests dressed in Colonial attire. The man seemed authentic in every respect, and they had enjoyed the show. Johnson, however, had not hired such a man, and he had not seen such a fellow at the party either.

In one room, a scuffle seems to occur periodically. According to Johnson, one afternoon he and a staff member were on the first floor, below the British Barracks Dining Room area, when they heard what sounded like someone throwing furniture around. The two men hurried upstairs because no one should have been up there, and it sounded as though someone was obviously damaging things. Upstairs, they found that tables were upended and chairs strewn around as if someone had knocked them over in a struggle. However, no one could be found on that floor.

Perhaps one of the strangest and most compelling stories about the General Wayne Inn came from a former patron of the restaurant. The guest testified that he had been in the coat check room reaching for his jacket when a black entity grabbed his hand. A terrible fear gripped the man as the spirit twisted him around and tried to force him to the ground. He felt as if the entity would murder him if it could get him down. The attack stopped abruptly, but the man never forgot his wrestling match with a ghost. It's the only report of anyone being touched or harmed by a spirit in the General Wayne Inn. The story would be easy to dismiss if not for the fact that the tale came from a very well-respected citizen.

At least one of the spirits in the building seems to enjoy pranks and making messes. A waiter set up a room for a wedding, carefully folding and tenting the napkins at each table to create a grand effect. When he returned the next morning to finish his preparations, the napkins were tossed about the room and he had to start over again.

The kitchen staff have reported similar incidents. A cook who was the last to leave the kitchen one afternoon left a stack of about twenty towels on a cabinet. The next morning, when he came in to open up for the day, he found the towels tossed all over the kitchen. No one had been in the building during the night because there had been a terrible snowstorm and the owner had closed up early. In fact, the cook and owner had left at the same time.

The bar seems to be one of the most haunted areas, with dozens of stories reported by the staff and patrons. One night the bartender was hurrying down the stairs to the basement to restock the liquor when he stopped short. Before him at the bottom of the stairs was a man in a Hessian uniform. The fellow turned back toward the basement and faded away. The bartender refused to ever go into the basement again; he'd give a liquor list to someone else to bring it up for him.

For months on end, between 3 and 4 P.M. each afternoon, the glasses hanging from the racks at the bar would tinkle and jingle as if someone were shaking them. The phenomenon stopped after a few months, but eventually it started up again.

Johnson came in one morning to find that the janitor had not completed his work. He was surprised because the man had always been very reliable, so he called to see if the man was okay. Had he gotten ill or been hurt? Why had he not completed his work? The janitor informed his boss that he had quit. It seems that while the janitor was working the night before, a Colonial soldier had appeared before him in the bar. The man had simply laid his broom down and left the building for the last time.

One day Johnson came into the bar and found that the cash register drawer was full of water when he opened it. He looked up and saw nearly thirty carafes filled with water; the water glasses on the shelves also were filled, and so was a wine rack that stood nearby. It looked as if someone had taken great pleasure in filling every available vessel with water. At first he was puzzled by the strange event. How could water get into the drawer, the carafes, and the glasses but not on the floor or anywhere else? There were no pipes above the bar, no leaks in the ceiling, and no one else around to have done it. The mystery compounded when Johnson tried to get the insurance company to pay for repairs to the electric cash register, which apparently had been shorted out. The company sent out a representative, who tried to find a rational explanation. None could be found, and the representative recommended that the company not pay for the machine repairs, although it finally agreed to pay half the repair price. Interestingly enough, Johnson later realized that this event was discovered the morning after voting day. He noticed that other odd events happened on that date too.

Perhaps one of the stranger phenomen at the bar is the neck blower. Johnson first noticed this. On busy nights when the bar was full, a woman at one end of the bar would suddenly react as if startled by something. She'd invariably turn to the man behind her and complain that he was blowing on her neck. As soon as the woman spoke, the next woman would have the same experience, and on up the bar it would go. Each lady would turn angrily to the man behind or beside her, and each man expressed ignorance of the events. This happened so often at one point that Johnson came to expect it on busy nights. Apparently one of the ghosts enjoyed teasing the ladies.

Johnson often told a story that might explain the flirting spirit. He said that during the Colonial period, a man who often frequented the tavern would annoy the ladies who worked there while he drank. One day he got terribly obnoxious with one of the young women, and a chivalrous man came to her rescue. The drunk insulted the young lady again, and a fight began, during which the drunkard was struck and killed. It is believed that this man is still flirting with and harassing the ladies.

In the early 1980s, a local television station came to Merion and filmed a segment about the ghosts of the General Wayne Inn. The owner and nearly fifty regular patrons gathered in the bar on the night of the broadcast to watch. As the segment started, the picture on the television began to slowly rotate clockwise until it had turned completely around. Again and again the picture slowly turned while that segment was on. The television never acted that way before or after the event. The owner later checked with the television station and friends, but everyone else saw it properly. Had the version on the bar television been altered by the spirits?

Not all of the spirits at the General Wayne Inn date from the Revolutionary War. Another famous entity thought to haunt the inn is none other than Edgar Allan Poe, who began visiting the General Wayne Inn in 1839. He made many of his trips with his dear friend and biographer, Henry Beck Hirst. It is known that Poe was an alcoholic and did some drugs. Some believe that Poe made his trips so that he could flee reality through drugs and drink in a place where he would not be well known or disturbed.

It is said that Poe had a favored seat near the window in the room where once Benjamin Franklin delivered the mail. Supposedly, Poe edited or wrote part of *The Raven* at that table and carved his initials into the glass window with a diamond ring that he borrowed for the purpose from Hirst. The window survived until the 1970s, when it was shattered by a jackhammer chiseling something outside. According to some reports, Poe has been glimpsed sitting at his favorite table still. Curiously, he has been seen in the building dressed not only in his customary suit, but also in his cadet's uniform. It is said that he seems tired, haggard, and worn. Other folks claim they have seen Edgar Allan Poe standing near a painting of him in the room, laughing at the picture and making fun of it.

Joseph Yoganski eventually purchased the General Wayne Inn from Johnson. When he first came to the building, he was well aware of the stories, but he did not really believe them. However, the spirits soon set about remedying that. One day Yoganski was changing lightbulbs in one of the chandeliers upstairs. After he had screwed in several bulbs and moved on to the next, something nearby caught his attention. He looked at the bulbs he had just screwed in, and they were unscrewing themselves one by one.

Yoganski had heard about the soldier in the basement, but he was not prepared to see the sight of a soldier walking through the basement visible only from his knees up. He later learned that some of the former staff had also seen this apparition that seems to be walking on the original floor of the basement, which has been raised about eighteen inches over time.

Through the years, the General Wayne Inn has drawn its share of psychics, some of whom may have contacted the spirits who reside at the inn. During a séance in the building, two sets of doors slammed shut when the medium began, and throughout the process, one of Johnson's adult sons claimed to see faces appearing briefly above the medium's head before fading away. The building was closed and locked, and everyone was gathered together in the same room.

Perhaps the most significant psychic event was when a man named Mr. Benio contacted Johnson. Benio said he had been having dreams in which a Hessian soldier kept begging him to come to the General Wayne Inn, telling him he wanted a proper burial. Intrigued, Johnson allowed Benio to visit the building. Benio came up with three names while there, saying that three different Hessians haunted the building. One was called Paul, another was Hans, but the third one would not give a name. Benio also reported seeing a young woman, who told him that as a maid there during the Revolution, she had been raped and killed in the building and was buried in the churchyard next door. Johnson was impressed, because he knew of such a story. The young woman was seen in the churchyard next door and also hurrying through the hall or fighting with some unseen force.

In recent years, the General Wayne Inn fell upon hard times. Then something happened that at first appeared to be a wonderful new start for the inn, but it quickly became a nightmare that might have spawned yet another ghost. In 1996, a successful pair of chefs, Guy Sileo and Jim Webb, took over the inn. The two were praised as great chefs with a creative and innovative way with American food. After successfully running a small restaurant that had received rave reviews, they had decided to move up to a much larger establishment, and they chose the General Wayne Inn. The inn had become shabby with time and lack of care, but the two thought they could restore the building and help it regain its reputation for good food, good drink, and good fun.

The task was much larger than they had anticipated, however, and soon they realized that they were sinking. Their response to the failure ultimately led to tragedy. Chef Webb wanted them to roll up their sleeves and redouble their efforts, salvaging what they could. Chef Sileo decided it was time to bail out. The two became increasingly hostile toward each other, which led to physical fights and terrible verbal rows. Webb began sleeping in his office on the third floor because he was working so many hours that he barely got any sleep, while Sileo was putting in far fewer hours.

On the morning of December 27, 1996, Sileo called the police. He had found his partner on the floor of his third-floor office dead. Webb had been shot in the back of the head.

While questioning the employees, the police learned that Sileo had been having an affair with a young sous chef named Felicia Moyse. Moyse indicated that Webb was becoming increasingly upset about the affair and had been causing trouble between the couple. Soon the police learned of a large insurance policy that the two chefs had taken out on each other. Sileo stood to inherit $650,000. Webb had also borrowed $100,000 from Sileo's father.

Felicia Moyse committed suicide soon after, and that only spurred speculation that she might have known or even helped with Webb's murder. It was obvious that this was a troubled young woman.

The police arrested and convicted Sileo for perjury. He later was indicted for Webb's murder.

The General Wayne Inn was sold to a real estate developer. There are already stories that the chef has returned to his kitchen, but these are only rumors so far.

The building has since been sold once again and is now slated to become a Jewish synagogue and restaurant. Will there be stories about the spirits in the future? The ghosts have been part of the building for a long time, and they likely will continue to be. It should only be a matter of time before new chapters are added to the long saga of the ghosts of the General Wayne Inn.

Eerie Bolton Mansion

Bolton Mansion sits—solid, sensible, and mute—on a hill now known as Holly Hill. It has an incredible tale to tell, but the gray stones from which the oldest part of the mansion was built give no sign of the history, love, and passion that its rooms witnessed.

Bolton Mansion was the second home in America built by Phineas Pemberton, a good friend of William Penn. The first home Pemberton built was on an estate of three hundred acres bordering

Penn's own estate. But the property was swampy bottom land, and Pemberton's first wife, his parents, and several of his children died during the 1690s from illnesses that he blamed on the wet land and weather conditions.

Pemberton decided to move his remaining family to a new home. He chose a site on a hill, calling it Holly Hill, and named his new home Bolton after his childhood home in England. He got married again, to a widow named Anne Harrison, and brought his new bride and her child to live with his family at Bolton. The couple had several children together and raised a large family at Bolton Mansion. As time and his finances permitted, he built onto his home.

Pemberton continued to represent William Penn's interests in the colony of Penns Woods. Upon Pemberton's death, Penn lamented the loss of a real friend and trusted business associate.

Through marriage, Bolton Mansion came into the hands of the politically and financially prominent Morris family, and the mansion's future was secured. The Morris family added onto and improved the house, which eventually had twenty-two rooms.

Before the Civil War, James Morris used the mansion as a stop on the Underground Railroad, building tunnels under the house that led to the river, where the slaves could board a boat and move onward to freedom. James was a socially prominent man who was appalled when his daughter Mary announced that she was in love with a man of low social status. He forbade Mary to see the young man again, but she was determined not to give up on her lover. She waited for the young man to return, but he never did. She grew more and more desperate and eventually hanged herself on the main staircase.

No one ever really knew what happened to the young man. Did he join the Army and die in battle? Did he just move on, or did the Morris family pay him to leave Mary alone? Those questions would remain for all time.

The tragic romance and death of Mary Morris spawned the main ghost stories at Bolton Mansion, but they were not the only ones. In fact, Mary's death was not the only suicide that took place in the house. Years later, a servant supposedly hanged himself by tying off a rope and jumping from a second-story bedroom window. No one ever knew why this man committed suicide.

The Morris family allowed Penn State to start an experimental farm at Bolton in 1938. The students lived in the house, and they raised various types of livestock in the barns and planted vegetables on the grounds. Students claimed to see a young woman coming down or hanging from the front stairs. They always just glimpsed the girl and never could see her when they looked for her directly. Others reported seeing a man hanging from the side of the house and a little girl looking out of a window. A woman was seen walking from the servants' area to the house early in the day. People began to believe it was the spirit of one of the servants returning daily for work. Some people also reported seeing black shadows moving and hearing faint whispering in the basement.

Bolton was then purchased by the United States Steel Company as housing for the men working on a project to build a new plant in the area. The men did not stay long, and the house was sold to William Levitt, founder of Levittown. Levitt bought a five-acre plot around the house—all that was left of the vast estate Phineas Pemberton had created. The original acreage had been divided again and again, and pieces of property had been sold off. Now only this comparatively small plot surrounding Bolton Mansion remained.

The Levitt family used the house for several years before giving it to Bristol Township, which used the house for municipal purposes. The building served as a courthouse and police headquarters, among other things. The township finally outgrew the building, and by the 1960s, abandoned and derelict, it was scheduled to be demolished. No one wanted Bolton Mansion anymore.

That was when a group of citizens from the area banded together as the Friends of Bolton Mansion to try to stop the wrecking ball. They knew nothing of the hauntings that had been associated with the old house. They managed to save the mansion from demolition, but restoration would take a long time.

Over the years, different group members and neighbors have reported odd experiences. Neighbors have said they saw a woman wearing a long dress and cloak walking around on the property at night. She captures people's attention because she glows softly in the dark. Another woman has been seen on the property who is crying and desperately looking for something, supposedly her lost child. It is not known who the woman may be, why her child is missing, or what happened to the child. Perhaps the little girl who haunts the second floor of the house is associated with the weeping woman outside. Neighbors and people visiting the house have reported seeing a little girl running from window to window on the second floor, peering out as if looking for someone.

Mary is also said to watch out the upstairs windows of Bolton Mansion. Perhaps even in death she is looking for her beloved.

The house has caught fire at least once, in the third-floor area where the children were housed. There are no records to indicate that anyone died in the blaze, but people often report feeling watched up there.

When the Friends of Bolton Mansion took over the property, they were faced with fire damage from another source, as the house had become a hangout for teens and vagrants. Some teens set the house on fire, and it damaged the interior significantly in places, but the old mansion did not burn down. Perhaps the spirits were protecting the property from vandals.

The basement of Bolton is split into two sections. The oldest part dates back three hundred years, and people often say that they do not feel alone in that area and are uncomfortable. On one side is a large stone fireplace, and people have glimpsed a woman who seems to be tending food there and then fades away quickly.

A second basement was built by James Morris before the Civil War. It is L-shaped, and the smaller part of the L has a crude dirt floor. That section is not illuminated by the lightbulb in the basement, and hidden in the darkness is the entrance to the tunnels. People have reported hearing a little girl singing near the entrance or seeing shadows moving and shifting back there. Once a paranormal group came to do an investigation in the mansion and found that the second basement was very active. They reported a child's hands touching one of the men in the room. Members of the group watched the infrared screen of their equipment in awe as the child's hands appeared up to the wrists. They also watched as a phantom child's hands plucked at the back of a member's shirt.

Perhaps an even more interesting investigation occurred in 1971, when Professor Don Gibson chose the mansion for an experiment he was conducting on paranoid reactions. Gibson's experiment was developed to observe people's reactions to a stressful and frightening situation. He chose Bolton because he felt it was a typical haunted house. He placed test subjects in various places and situations and had them observed by his team.

Professor Gibson later wrote a report about his experiment. He was most critical about the subjects and their reactions until he came to the question of whether the house was haunted. He stated that he and his team had experienced equipment failures and wrote, "We can't even begin to figure out a rational explanation for the equipment malfunctions. Electrical equipment can break down, and transporting it could cause damage to it, but items such as stethoscopes stopped working in the mansion and then worked again back at the lab."

The test subjects and observers noted other strange events as well. People in the experiment said they saw a woman who was looking for a child. They also felt as though they were being watched on the second floor. The test subjects were broken up into small groups and were not allowed to associate before or during the test. They were given no information about the house or hauntings there, yet the groups consistently reported the same feelings, impressions, and experiences throughout the building.

Perhaps one of the most interesting things to ever occur at Bolton Mansion was when some infrared photographs were taken in the building. In one shot of the main staircase, it appears as if a woman in a long dress is coming down the stairs. Another photo shows what appears to be a man's pant leg with a wide stripe like a Union Army outfit would have had. Perhaps the photos were of young Mary and her beau, who joined the Army during the Civil War and finally has come back for her.

The Specters of Baleroy Mansion

The Chestnut Hill section of Philadelphia is filled with old mansions, grand gardens, and the charm of a bygone era. Standing out among the other mansions is a home known as Baleroy Mansion. With ornamental cresting, a domed turret, and a mansard roof, the house is bound to draw attention. But it is known for more than its beautiful architecture: It is thought to be one of the most haunted houses in the United States, and perhaps the most haunted in Pennsylvania.

By historical standards, the house is not that old. Built in 1911, the thirty-three-room mansion was sold a dozen years later to the parents of the current owner, George Meade Easby. The only remaining family member, Easby is a direct descendant of his namesake, General George Meade, who won fame in the Civil War at the Battle of Gettysburg.

George Meade Easby's parents bought the house in 1926 when he was six years old. George and his five-year-old brother, Steven, found the mansion fascinating. Such a large house with its many hiding places and interesting turns was a haven for the boys. One of the features they liked best was the great fountain in the front courtyard. It was a large, grand affair, and the brothers enjoyed gazing into its waters.

Boys are naturally drawn to water, so George and Steven often played near the fountain. One day the boys were watching the rippling waters and how it warped their reflections, when suddenly little George stared into the water in horror. Steven's reflection had suddenly twisted into a horrible skeleton head. George gasped at the grinning skull, but as suddenly as it had appeared, the skeleton head reflection gave way to Steven's little face once again. For George, that skull was more than troubling. Little did he know it then, but he had seen a portent of his brother's fate.

About a month later, little Steven came down with a childhood illness and soon died. But according to Easby, his little brother has not yet left the house and seems to be keeping George company to this day.

Many incidents over the years have convinced George that his little brother is still at Baleroy. One evening during a dinner party, the guests heard a crash come from the gallery. George and his guests hurried up to see what had happened. They found that a picture of Steven had seemed to have flung itself nearly fifteen feet across the room. George picked up the picture and saw that the wire on the frame was still intact. He and some of his guests then examined the wall where the picture had hung, and the hook was still in place too. Reason told him that the picture could not have just come off the hook without something having broken. Furthermore, if the picture had simply fallen, it would have landed near the wall, but this picture had been tossed across the gallery. George thought perhaps Steven was playing one of the pranks he has become known for.

On another occasion when George had guests, a copper pot suddenly launched itself off the shelf and struck a guest in the head. The guest was more shocked than hurt, and George brushed it off as another of his little brother's pranks.

Perhaps one of the best confirmations of Steven's presence came from two contractors who were doing some restoration work on the property. One day the men were working in the foyer near the fountain when they felt as if they were enveloped by cold air. Feeling compelled to look up, they both saw a young boy with blond hair watching them work. The men knew there were no young children at Baleroy. They told George Easby of their experience and described the child, whom he immediately recognized as his brother, Steven.

George's mother, Henrietta, also seems to have returned to her home. Over the years, George has shared his paranormal playground with many people, among them psychic Judith Haimes. Judith has visited the mansion many times, and she was not surprised by the number of spirits there. One evening, she began to hear a woman saying, "Longfellow, Longfellow, Longfellow . . ." over and over again. She didn't think this made any sense, so she kept this to herself throughout dinner. However, the voice persisted and then began to include the phrase "the children's hour . . ."

Now Judith felt compelled to speak up. She asked George if the words made any sense to him. Indeed, they did. His mother's favorite author had been Henry Wadsworth Longfellow, and her favorite poem was "The Children's Hour." George and Judith took this to mean that his mother, Henrietta, was coming through for some reason.

Still, they could not figure out why Mrs. Easby was repeating the phrase. Judith eventually went home, and George retired to his study to do some reading. As he sat and rested, he noticed that a book on one of the shelves was pulled out as if someone had been looking at the title but forgot to push it back into the stacks. George got up to push the book back into place, but he froze when he saw the title of the book. It was a tome of poems by Henry Wadsworth Longfellow.

He reached out tentatively and touched the book. He felt compelled to take it down. The book was dusty with age and lack of

use, but he brushed off the dust and opened it up. An old envelope was tucked into the book, right at the page with the poem "The Children's Hour." On the envelope was his mother's handwriting: "To my son Meade in the event of my death." George hastened to open the envelope but was dismayed when he found it empty.

However, Henrietta was not to be thwarted that easily. She opened up communications with her son through Judith. One day, following Henrietta's direction, Judith led George to the house's storeroom, where she said his mother told her she had hidden a pair of silver candlesticks in the rafters. George searched where Judith said to look and soon came up with the candlesticks.

Another day, Henrietta directed Judith to tell her son one of the desks in the old house had a secret drawer. In the drawer, they found a bullet-torn and gunpowder-smudged old Confederate flag that had been captured by General George Meade at the battle of Gettysburg. The flag was a precious family heirloom.

Henrietta seemed bent upon unearthing all of the family's secrets for George, and she continued to direct him through Judith. One afternoon, George and Judith went to the attic on Henrietta's direction. Once there, Judith quickly located a trunk that Henrietta wanted them to search. They quickly found the document George's mother was so insistent that he find—an old promissory note from the early 1800s. The document proved that George's great-great-grandfather, Richard Meade, had loaned the fledgling federal government $5 million in 1819 to help defray the costs of annexing Florida from Spain.

George looked into the matter and learned that the federal government had never honored the note. He was due that money as well as more than 170 years of interest on the loan. He began the legal work to receive the money his family was due.

Throughout the years, George Easby came to realize that his home was a very haunted place. There seemed to be no reason why so many ghosts were in the house. The property did not have a history of being haunted before the Easbys bought it, but perhaps most of the spirits there came along with the many treasured antiques that furnish the home.

Among the specters at Baleroy is the spirit of an elderly woman who had been seen hobbling along the second floor with a cane. George has also spotted a monk in tan robes and later came to learn that in his ancestral home in Europe, his family was associated with a group of monks who wore tan robes. And a tall grandfather clock in the house seems to draw the spirit of Thomas Jefferson or a man who looks amazingly like him.

Another spirit at Baleroy should not be trifled with. Her name is Amanda, and she seems to have come to Baleroy along with an antique chair that is in the Blue Room. Amanda is a malicious spirit and has been blamed for several deaths.

One night, George awoke when he felt someone grab his arm in a painfully hard grip. It took him a few seconds to realize that he was alone with an invisible force that held him captive. He had little doubt that this was not a dream, and in the morning, dark fingerprint bruises appeared on his arm. George believed that it was the malicious spirit of Amanda holding him down.

One of the most troubling things about Amanda is that she is alleged to have killed at least three people who have visited Baleroy, one of whom was a dear friend and employee of George's. When the psychic Judith Haimes first visited the house, George asked his employee Paul Kimmons to show her around. Kimmons had worked for George for several years and simply did not believe the ghost stories. He had never had an encounter in the house, so he had no reason to believe in the ghosts. He was most cordial to Judith, however, and walked her through the entire mansion. He answered her questions, offered up fascinating bits of information about the many beautiful objects in the house.

As they were walking, Kimmons suddenly stopped dead. Before them was a blue mist, which he knew was associated with sightings of Amanda. The mist wafted down the front stairs and came toward the pair before dissipating. Kimmons was terribly shaken by the event. It was a life-altering experience for the man who did not believe in spooks and specters. Judith Haimes tried to comfort her companion, but he was very distraught.

A few weeks after the tour, Judith received a phone call from a very troubled Paul Kimmons, who insisted that the spirit from Baleroy named Amanda had followed him home. His voice was anxious and tired as related his experiences since the day of the sighting. As he drove home that day, he looked into his rearview mirrow and saw Amanda sitting in his backseat. When he looked directly into the backseat, he could see nothing, but in the mirror, he could see Amanda clearly. After that, Kimmons said that he constantly saw Amanda wherever he went. She'd catch his eye in a crowd. She'd wake him up by standing over him at night. He could not shake her.

Kimmons grew more tired and desperate over the following month. He insisted that Amanda was with him everywhere he went. As George Easby watched on, his friend and employee grew more and more haggard and distraught. The last time George saw Paul Kimmons alive, he had come into the Blue Room and found Kimmons slouched back in the antique chair that belonged to Amanda, fitfully sleeping as if in the middle of an unpleasant dream. George left the room quietly.

A couple days later, George was notified that Paul Kimmons was dead. For George Easby, it was a terrible thing. He had lost a trusted employee and friend. He believed that Amanda was somehow responsible for hounding his employee to death. He was also terribly concerned, because Paul Kimmons was the third person who had sat in Amanda's chair and died only days later. George believed that somehow sitting in the chair helped cause the deaths of those three people.

The chair has become known as the "death chair," and George has since draped a cord over it so that no one can sit in it. Anyone who is daring enough to try must first listen to the stories of the three people who died after sitting in it. Usually the stories are enough to convince them that they should not anger Amanda.

Paul Kimmons was not the first person to see Amanda. In fact, the study is called the Blue Room because the blue mist associated with Amanda has been seen in there so often. Usually the mist has been seen hovering around the antique chair, and no sightings of the mist were reported before the chair came into the house.

Another friend of George's also had a run-in with the mist, but his encounter did not end so badly. Lloyd Gross was skeptical of the tales of Amanda and the other ghosts of Baleroy. An antique dealer, he had been friends with George Easby for many years and had heard all the tales but scoffed at them. One day, George asked Gross to take a reporter who was doing a story about Baleroy and its paranormal inhabitants through the house on a tour. Gross obliged his friend, but he did not play up any of the paranormal tales.

As the two men stood in a room talking, the reporter's tape recorder flew from his hand and landed on the ground nearly twenty feet away. Gross turned in shock to see why the man had thrown his equipment. The reporter, however, was terribly frightened and gasped out an impossible story. He had just been standing there, he said, when something grabbed the recorder from his hand. The reporter was so upset that he refused to stay and finish the tour. He had gotten more ghost stories than he had bargained for.

Even the incident with the reporter did not convince Gross that Baleroy was truly haunted, but he could no longer deny the spirits after he met Amanda. One day he was helping George prepare the house for a charity event, when he glanced up to see a thick blue mist form and drift out of the Blue Room. At first he did not realize what he was seeing. He pointed out the mist to George, saying it must be getting cold out.

George Easby took one look at the mist and shook his head, explaining that it was the ghost. Gross could not find any rational reason for the blue mist that came from the Blue Room.

George was grateful that nothing seemed to have happened to his friend other than a bit of a scare. That night, after the charity event, the two men were walking down the driveway toward Gross's car when the antique dealer suddenly stopped and spun to confront his friend, demanding to know why George had struck him. Even as he said the words, both men realized that George had been much too far away to have reached his friend. This was Gross's second paranormal experience in one day. George feared that Amanda was at work.

His fears were confirmed later that night, when his friend told him that on arriving at home, he saw a blue mist in his front room through the window. Anger and fear mingled as Gross unlocked the front door and charged into his living room. The mist faded away and left a terribly shaken man behind. Gross was no longer a skeptic. He now believed in ghosts—at least those of Baleroy.

The grounds are also said to be haunted—by a phantom car. People repeatedly have heard a car pulling up the long driveway to the house. The car sounds as if it is stopping just before the front door, but no one ever comes in. When someone goes to check, they find nothing. A few people claim to have seen a long car from the

1930s pull past the windows. When they hurried to the door to get a better look, the car vanished before their astonished eyes.

It is easy to see why Baleroy has earned a reputation as one of the most haunted houses in the nation.

Eastern State Penitentiary

In 1787, a group of men from Philadelphia gathered in Benjamin Franklin's home to discuss the inhumane conditions of their prisoners. Until that date, the prisons were designed for punishment and were horrible hell holes. The men gathered that night embraced the Quaker tenet of repenting and thus created a new type of prison and a new word—penitentiary. They envisioned a place of quiet solitude where men and women could reflect on their sins, repent of their misdeeds, and be released as good citizens. But what they actually created was a new form of hell.

In 1829, the Eastern State Penitentiary was opened. A modern marvel, the building was the most expensive ever constructed in the United States up to that time. Architect John Haviland originally designed the prison to hold 250 prisoners in single-person cells, but he was forced to modify it to hold 450. Simple and clever, the plan was known as a wagon wheel design. The center of the prison complex was the hub, and the wings ran off the hub like spokes in a wheel. The beauty of this design was that the guards could watch all of the prison wings from the central hub.

The prison also had some revolutionary design ideas. It was the first public building to have indoor plumbing and running water in each cell. Even the president did not have flush toilets in the White House, but Eastern State Penitentiary had them in every cell. The septic pipes were run alongside the water pipes, however, and when the boilers heated the water, it also inadvertently heated the pipes, filling the entire building with an awful stench. The fetid air was only one of the many problems with the building.

The cells were entered by way of narrow, short doors designed to make the prisoners bend over, so that they would bow and remember to be humble. Each cell was equipped with a small skylight in the ceiling as the only source of light. The skylight was known as the "Eye of God" and was designed to make the prisoner cast his eyes heavenward.

The prison was in many respects built like a grand cathedral. It had great vaulted ceilings, skylights in the aisles, and grand arched walkways. It was meant to be a place for repentance and reflection. The Quakers hoped that the solitude would induce the inmates to think better of their ways and grow closer to God.

The prisoners, both men and women, were brought into the building, where they were physically examined. In a great book, their physical condition, identifying marks, and even the length of their feet were recorded. It was determined whether the person could read and write, and that was noted. The person was then given an outfit with numbers sewn on it and was then forced to have a black hood put over the head. Prisoners were led from the room to their cells in total darkness. The inmate would not see where he was or see any of the other inmates, and even most of the guards would only be shadows from then on. The person was now reduced to a number. He would work, eat, sleep, and spend every moment of his time in that small cell until his sentence was up.

The prisoners lived in near total isolation. But beyond the isolation was the total silence of their world. They were not permitted to talk—even to themselves. They could not whistle, sing, tap, or make any sound. The guards even wore socks over their shoes in order to subdue the sound of their footfalls. The intent was to force the prisoners to spend all of their time reflecting on their circumstances. They were not allowed any books other than the Bible, nor were they allowed any contact with the outside world or their own families.

Despite the lofty goals that had created the prison, this treatment was immensely cruel. People were driven mad in the confines of the little stone cells. Mental illness was a constant problem.

In Eastern State Penitentiary, any infraction of the rules could elicit harsh punishment. Prisoners could be stripped naked and left without blankets in the cold, tomblike, stone cells, even in the winter months.

But worse punishments awaited unrepentant prisoners. The water bath was an idea taken from insane asylums and twisted to be even more cruel. Prisoners were stripped and doused with ice water. On occasion, they were chained outside and doused with ice water during the winter. Ice would freeze on their skin. They would be left in this condition for some time, and then the ice-water treatments were reapplied. Later, prisoners were chained to the outside walls of the prison and pelted with high-pressure water. The pain was intense, but the treatment left no marks.

Another favorite punishment used by the prison guards was to chain up inmates in dark cells. Often they were stripped of clothing and given no blankets. They were given half rations of bread and water only. There are stories of prisoners who spent nearly two months in these conditions. In one account, a counselor was fired for giving water to a delirious prisoner who had been in a dark cell for forty-two days and was teetering on mental and physical collapse.

Inmates were also bound by chains and leather straps in a "mad chair," where they were kept for hours or even days. Their limbs would swell and turn black, and they would be crippled when released.

Sometimes a straitjacket-type device would be placed on an inmate, who would be forced to endure this for hours or days. The jacket was so tight that it cut off circulation to the neck and head and the prisoner often passed out. When he was unbound, the pain was immense.

But the punishment that the prisoners feared the most was the iron gag, a five-inch metal piece that fit over the prisoner's tongue. The prisoner was cuffed with his wrists behind him, and a chain was connected between the gag and the handcuffs. If the prisoner moved or struggled in any way, the gag cut painfully into his mouth. The cuts and mangling of the mouth were terrible to behold, and at least one inmate died from this punishment.

By the beginning of the industrial revolution, the prison administration realized they had a great resource. Private contractors leased the prison labor, providing the materials and training and making a great profit from the cheap workforce. The leasing out of labor led to the abandonment of the policy of total isolation. Prison shops were set up to do the work more efficiently, and the inmates were permitted to speak, but only about the work at hand.

From nearly the beginning, there were charges of corruption and graft within the prison, along with stories of every possible type of abuse to the inmates. The prison had many critics, chief among them author Charles Dickens, who visited the prison on a tour of the United States. He returned to England and wrote about what he had learned from speaking to the prisoners and observing the techniques at the prison. "I hold this slow and daily tampering with the mysteries of the brain," he said, "to be immeasurably worse than any torture of the body."

But not everyone was critical of the prison. In fact, at one time nearly ten thousand people a year toured the prison, and during its heyday, seventeen hundred inmates were housed there. What came to be known as the Pennsylvania System was applauded by other corrections departments, and three hundred prisons around the world eventually were designed based on Eastern State Penitentiary.

Ghost stories started to circulate long before the prison shut down in 1971. One of the most famous began during the eight months when mobster Al Capone was incarcerated there for carrying concealed weapons on a visit to Philadelphia shortly after the St. Valentine's Day Massacre. Capone is believed to have ordered the murder of the Moran gang in a Chicago garage on that holiday. Among those gunned down was a man named James Clark.

Accounts indicate that Capone was given a large room in the prison with a desk and lamps. While in the prison, he was allowed to meet not only with his lawyers, but also with business associates. The same accounts state that Capone believed that James Clark was haunting him and that he was often heard pleading with the man to leave him alone. He was later convicted of income tax evasion and sent to Alcatraz Island, where the guards also stated that Capone often pleaded with Clark to leave him alone. Capone was beginning to suffer from dementia as a result of an untreated case of syphilis, but his valet, Hymie Cornish, also claimed to have seen Clark's restless spirit, and Capone's bodyguards broke into his suite back in Chicago many times thinking that someone was in the room hurting Capone. Each time, however, they found Capone alone and very upset because "Jimmy" had been there after him.

During the last years of Eastern State Penitentiary's use, many prisoners and guards claimed to have had paranormal encounters. Stories of phantom screams, ghostly footsteps, and specters were nearly commonplace.

In 1971, the building was designated a national historic landmark and sold to the city of Philadelphia as a possible tourist site. The Pennsylvania Prison Society of Philadelphia took over and began promoting the prison, offering tours. As the tourists came and tour guides worked there, more phenomena were reported.

Many people talked about seeing black shadows moving among the ruins of the old prison and hearing footsteps, screams, talking voices, and laughter coming from various cells.

Today a walk through the prison is like stepping back in time. Paint is peeling, and the damp walls and dank air seem to invite spirits. Old furniture appears to await the dead, and even the desks still have papers inside them as if the guards are only on break. There are areas where the staff and tourists consistently report experiences. Cell Blocks Six and Twelve, Death Row, the Infirmary, and the Central Guard Tower all have their own tales to be told.

Cell Block Six and the other old cell blocks seem to house shadowy figures who move among the ruins. People have repeatedly reported seeing someone going into a cell, only to find no one there when they reached the cell. In Cell Block 12, disembodied laughter has been reported from some of the cells. Brave souls have looked for the source of the crazy laughter, but no reasonable explanation has ever been found. Death Row was the cell block where prisoners waited to be transferred to meet "Old Sparky." People have seen a shadowy black figure running down the hall, darting from cell to cell. Others say they heard voices whispering in the cells as they passed by.

The Infirmary leaves people feeling shaken and watched. They report hearing voices and screams, but no one is ever seen. Through the years, various paranormal groups have reported capturing voices in the Infirmary. In the Central Guard Tower, a ghostly guard has been observed still keeping watch over the prison. Several people have reported seeing this guard walking his tour and surveying the prison from his lofty overlook.

Perhaps the most famous modern story is that of locksmith Gary Johnson, who was working on some rusted locks in one of the cell blocks and kept feeling as if he were being watched. He tried to keep his mind on his work, but the feeling was so intense that he kept looking up to check the hallway, expecting to see someone watching him, but no one was visible. Finally he saw a black shadow jump across the hallway toward him. Shaken, he left the area hurriedly.

Through the years, many movies, documentaries, and television shows were filmed inside the old prison. Ghost groups and tourists have spent nights within the confines of the walls, and many have come out with their own stories to tell. Among the moldy ruins of the prison, remnants that witnessed nearly two hundred years of anger, torture, and madness, people say that spirits are still lingering. It may be that some have stayed to guard, others await release, and still others remain because that was where they went mad. If any place in Pennsylvania is haunted, it would be Eastern State Penitentiary, where the dead seem to have taken over the prison.

Waiting for the Last Curtain Call

The State Theater Center for the Arts in Easton is a preservation and restoration success story. A small theater was built on the site in 1910, followed by a larger one in 1925 designed by Philadelphia architect W. L. Lee. Inspired by the Davanzanti Palace in Florence, Italy, and by old Spanish architecture, he employed local Italian artisans in creating beautiful frescoes and gilding. After the vaudeville era, the theater gained a large movie screen and sound equipment and showed movies from the 1930s until the 1960s. It was during that time period that J. Fred Osterstock managed the company that owned the theater. During a flood in 1955, Osterstock, described as a "distinguished-looking gentleman," actually lived at the State Theater, making the office to the right of the foyer his home.

In the 1970s, the magnificent frescoes were covered over with paint, and the theater was used for rock concerts. It was during this time period that stories of strange sightings began.

A couple maintenance workers were finishing up their chores hours after patrons had emptied the theater. They were about to leave the stage area when they caught a glimpse of a man at the back of the theater, just standing there as if observing that everything was being done correctly. As they walked to confront him, he vanished, and the workers could find no one else in the theater. Another time, they saw the figure entering one of the utility closets. When the workers opened the door, no one was there. Once his presence was so substantial that they called the police. But a thorough investigation of the entire building revealed no one.

Later the mysterious presence was seen again by the workers, and they called the police a second time. This time the officers brought dogs. Some believe that animals are more sensitive to paranormal entities, perhaps because the entities have electromagnetic properties that affect the large amount of fur on the animals similarly to when the hair on the back of a person's neck stands up. Sure enough, the dogs reacted to something in the theater. They appeared to sense someone near, and their hackles rose, but no one could be seen.

It is believed that the entity is the ghost of J. Fred Osterstock, the loyal manager who perhaps has taken his job a little too seriously. Historian Ken Klabunde, in the late 1970s, watched as someone walked off the empty stage while he was closing the theater for the evening. Later, in his research, he discovered a photograph of the man whom he had seen walk off the stage. It was Osterstock. He has been seen at least ten times, often by members of the State Theater's board of directors.

In 1981, the theater was threatened with demolition, but a coalition of concerned citizens, called the Friends of the State Theater, was formed and raised the funds to save it. They created a nonprofit organization, and the city of Easton donated a grant for researching development possibilities. They eventually raised enough money for restoration, and live performances began again in the historic State Theater and continue to this day. In 2002, the theater wanted to start a program to recognize local high school performers, sort of their own version of the Oscars. They named it the Freddy Awards, after the eternally caring manager who loved the State Theater too much to ever leave.

The Haunted Library

Libraries have always been places of refuge where you can lose yourself among the written thoughts of some of the world's greatest minds and escape into another world. They are normally places of quiet solitude. And so it is with the Public Library in Easton. Or at least, that's the way it should be, but for the nagging, repeated experiences of some of the patrons and staff.

Imagine sitting at one of the library's desks, deeply engrossed in your reading. One of the staff has just quieted a group of students across the room and passes you with a smile. A few seconds later, you assume she returned, for someone touches your shoulder. You turn, thinking you'll see her standing behind you . . . but no one is there.

Or your pleasant mood is shattered by a loud crash from some books that fell to the floor nearby. Startled, you look around for the culprit who threw the books off the shelves, but you prove to be alone on that floor of the library.

Or you're poring over the volumes on one of the shelves, looking for just the right book for some light summer reading. Suddenly, unseen hands tousle your hair.

You relate your experiences under your breath to one of the librarians and discover that they are not unusual at all—that actually, you're lucky more hasn't happened. She tells you about the time the filing cabinet drawers flew open, all by themselves. And you wonder about the strange, sharp sound you heard when you were back in the stacks when she tells you of the doors in the library that slam shut, then swing open again, all of their own accord.

Well, while you are in the library, you might decide to try to do a little research on the Easton Public Library itself. If you do, you may discover a few things that make you wish you hadn't started digging. Your research will unveil that in 1903, during the excavation for the construction of the building, workers began to unearth something bizarre: bodies. And the more they kept digging, the more they found, 514 in all. Most of the bodies were moved to other cemeteries. Thirty went unclaimed.

Two of the bodies, because of their stature in life, were given prominent reburial sites. Elizabeth Bell "Mammy" Morgan was reinterred in the library's west lawn and William Parsons in the front lawn. Since then, there have been reports of a figure, the mere shadow of a woman, moving with a strange, almost floating motion across the library grounds. It is said that this is "Mammy" Morgan's wraith, who drifts about the grounds at night, apparently unsettled about her exhumation and reburial under the west lawn.

Even more chilling, the bodies of the unknown, as well as the numerous unattached body parts that were unearthed, were reburied *en masse* in a vault located under the library's northeast driveway—an area that the dead seem to want to reclaim, since the driveway's been settling into a depression ever since.

Rain Boy

Jack Rundle first heard of Donnie Decker at the Strausburg Police Station, where he was an officer in the early 1980s. Jack worked the 4 P.M. to midnight shift, and some of the day officers were talking about a strange call they had received. They told Jack that a family named Keefer had reported some strange occurrences in their home since they had taken in a street kid named Donnie Decker to help straighten him out. The boy had had some minor brushes with the law, but he had never been in any serious trouble.

Donnie Decker, a big boy who looked as if he might one day become overweight, had been raised by his grandfather. The man had abused him a great deal, but Donnie had kept the abuse to himself. His grandfather had recently died, and Donnie seemed angry and depressed and got into trouble with the law. No one understood at that point that Donnie was not dealing with grief over the loss of his grandfather, but with the death of his secret abuser and the guilt that it brought. The boy was at a turning point in his life, and the Keefers knew Donnie and hoped to make a difference in his life.

The family had called the police, however, because they insisted that "strange happenings" were going on in Donnie's presence. The Keefers were frightened and wanted some help. They said that when the boy was in their house, droplets of water would appear from nowhere. In effect, they were claiming that when Donnie Decker was in the house, it rained around him.

Jack Rundle and a fellow officer decided to stop by the house to investigate. Jack didn't know what was going on, but he suspected that Donnie was having some fun at the family's expense. Jack was not a man who was easily fooled, and he thought they would spend a little time at the Keefer house and sort the thing out.

The Keefers were a nice family, but they didn't have a lot of money. Their house was an old wooden duplex, with three rooms on each floor and a single bathroom on each side. Jack and the other officer quickly learned how Donnie had come to live with the family. The Keefers and Donnie told a strange tale, however, of rain materializing out of nowhere, as well as other bizarre events.

While they watched, rain seemed to fall inside the house where Donnie was. Jack noted, however, that the rain always fell sideways. It did not come down from the ceiling, but from the side of the room away from Donnie. The rain came toward him very slowly. Jack could actually see it coming at the boy before it hit. Jack examined the rain and found that the droplets were large and sort of oily, but they didn't seem to last long. When they evaporated, there was no residue. It was one of the strangest things he had ever seen, and he made note of the situation.

Each day for several days, Jack and another officer would go down to the house where Donnie was staying. Over time, he witnessed several events that he could not explain. One afternoon, the rain was slanting across the room and soaking everything on the other side. Jack glanced down at a coffee table that was coated with water. Something was odd about it. On the table lay the family Bible, and it suddenly struck Jack that the water was coating everything on the table except the Bible. He reached out to touch it, and although everything else on the table was covered with the slightly oily liquid, the Bible was completely dry. Jack looked up at Donnie, but the boy was not doing anything to make it happen.

On another day, Jack and other officers were at the house observing events. Donnie was standing near Jack when suddenly he began to scream and tear at the T-shirt he was wearing. "It's burning me!" Donnie shouted. "It's burning me!" He grabbed at something around his neck and ripped it off. As it hit the ground, Jack saw that it was a cross on a chain. Donnie tore his shirt off as Jack picked up the necklace. To his surprise, it was very hot. In fact, he would later say that it was as hot as if it had been held over a fire. When Jack looked up at Donnie, he was shocked to see a cross burned on the boy's chest. The burn was fresh, and Jack could not explain it.

By now, Jack was convinced that whatever was happening at the house was not normal. He did not necessarily like Donnie, who seemed to be a bit of a screwup, but he also felt sorry for the boy. Some of the officers were saying that somehow Donnie was doing this himself, but those men had not been in the house when the things happened. Jack was certain that Donnie was not causing the events—at least, not in any natural way.

Jack could not imagine anything weirder than being pelted by this oily water and seeing the boy burned by the cross on a neckchain, but he was about to witness an even more bizarre and aggressive event. One afternoon, Jack and the other officers were in the house when Donnie Decker gave out a shout. The boy was levitated off the floor. He hung suspended in the air for a few seconds and then was slammed into a wall. The boy fell to the floor and just stayed there. The officers rushed up to him and examined his condition. The boy was shaken, winded, and frightened. He was still gasping for air, and Jack saw puncture wounds on his neck. They were not regular finger marks, and no one could come up with a reasonable explanation for how they had gotten there. Jack had spoken to Donnie only seconds before he had been grabbed up, and he knew for certain that the bloody wounds had not been on his neck at that time.

Another afternoon when Jack got to the police station, he spoke to one of the sergeants who had also been to the Keefer home. The sergeant was convinced that whatever was happening around Donnie Decker was spiritual in nature. He was a devout Catholic, and after witnessing an attack on Donnie, the officer had run down the street to a Catholic church and spoke to the priests about the events. None of the priests would go to the house with him, but one of them did give him some holy water in a little clear bottle. The priest instructed the sergeant to take the water back and sprinkle it around the room where the rain and other phenomena were occurring.

The sergeant took the water back to the Keefer house and started to sprinkle it around the room with Donnie and the rain. As soon as he began, something seemed to happen to the holy water in the bottle. The water grew milky like old dishwater. As the sergeant kept sprinkling the water, it got thick like skimmed milk, and then the bottle grew hot. The sergeant was a big man, but he had never encountered anything that had frightened him so much, and he was very shaken by the experience.

On another afternoon, between 4:30 and 5 P.M., Donnie went to the kitchen for something to eat. By now, Jack had seen a pattern emerge. The activity around Donnie started about that same time every afternoon. Jack and his fellow officer heard a banging and clanging from the kitchen. They hurried in to find Donnie standing in the middle of the room. Pots and pans were hanging on hooks on the wall, and they were banging themselves around. Donnie just stood and stared at the antics of the pans; he was too far away to have manipulated them. Jack could not find any way to make the pans react in the same way later on.

Yet another afternoon, Jack and some fellow officers were called to the house because the rain had gotten worse. As he stood looking at the room, something struck him. The raindrops seemed to materialize across the room and slant at him from that angle. At the moment that the drops materialized, they glowed slightly with an almost neon light. As the drops struck him, he looked down at his left arm. That afternoon he was wearing his leather police jacket, and the drops were clearly visible on it. He was amazed to see that the rain was rolling up his sleeve and not down. It was as if the rules of nature were twisted at that moment. He clearly observed rain materializing and raining sideways and then upward. Nothing about the events made any sense.

Jack and his fellow officers were not the only ones outside the family to witness these manifestations. A local schoolteacher and family friends also saw the strange rain and the attacks.

Soon word began to leak out, and the press got involved. The police chief forbade the officers to speak to the press about the matter. It didn't really matter to Jack. He was more interested in figuring out what was happening.

When Jack looked back on all this later, he was surprised at how calm everyone in the force had been about what was going on. There was little buzz about it, and the men rarely mentioned it to each other. He puzzled about why no one ever tried to seriously investigate the events. The police did come and witness different attacks, but they never really took over.

Eventually a local photographer who was intrigued by the paranormal began to look into the matter. His name was Chip Decker, no relation to Donnie. He collected eyewitness accounts, took photographs of the people and events, and began to gather whatever evidence he could

A couple months after the strange events began, Donnie was arrested for a petty crime and placed in the local county jail. There matters grew even more bizarre. Warden Dave Keenhold, a corrections officer at the Monroe County Prison, got to know Donnie Decker well during his stay there.

Warden Keenhold first heard about Donnie when officers and some of the inmates began to complain that the boy was spitting water at them. Upon questioning, the warden found that no one ever saw Donnie spitting, but it was the only rational explanation they could come up with.

The simple solution seemed to be to move Donnie. Maybe he would give up his antics, or else he could be sanctioned and made to stop them. Dave Keenhold worked the 3 to 11 P.M. shift, and helped move Donnie from the old jail to the new modular section. He hoped that this would be enough to stop Donnie's annoying little habit.

One evening, Dave was talking about Donnie to another officer, who voiced his opinion that the boy was kind of strange. They discussed the boy's claim that it would rain on anyone. Dave thought that Donnie was just doing this for attention.

Later that evening, the other officer had to go into the cell block area to see Donnie, whom he greeted as he did the other prisoners. He asked Donnie about the water that seemed to constantly be around him.

"How do you do it, Donnie?" the officer asked.

Donnie got up and walked close to the bars. "I can control it," he said.

The officer challenged, "Then make it rain on Dave; he's at the booking desk."

Donnie smiled at him. "Okay, it's raining on him. Go check."

The officer went back to the booking desk. Dave was sitting there working. He had on a clean new shirt that he had just put on for the first time that day. The other officer called Dave over to the door and said excitedly, "Look at your shirt."

Dave looked down. "What the heck is this? I just put this on," he said, feeling the large splotch of water on his new shirt. The moisture felt oily, like silicone. Donnie Decker was fifteen feet away, in another room and behind bars, but somehow he had made it rain on Dave. Dave was truly shaken and did not want to talk about it. This brush with Donnie Decker began what would be three months of nightmares for Dave.

By now the words "demonically possessed" had entered the vocabulary of those around Donnie. Dave could not help but worry that something from his encounters would follow him home to harm his children. He was not the only person who was worried about that scenario, and he would not find the coming events very reassuring.

It seemed that the boy was truly troubled, and no matter where he went, this moisture surrounded him. It coated the walls, puddled on the floor, and misted around him. He was wet, the objects in the room were wet, and Donnie seemed to enjoy his ability. Dave noted that the water dried clear and evaporated much more quickly than regular water did.

Eventually Dave decided to call on the prison chaplain, Reverend Blackburn, to talk to Donnie. Reverend Blackburn was not the full-time chaplain of the prison; in fact, he was just filling in when he first got the call to come and speak to an inmate. Dave knew the minister to be a good man and hoped that the reverend might be able to guide Donnie and diffuse the situation.

Reverend Blackburn arrived one evening and shook off his overcoat before entering the cell. He laid the overcoat down and picked up his Bible. The minister sat down and began to talk to Donnie. Suddenly the moisture began. It came from nowhere, and the luminous drops moved so slowly that the preacher could see them coming. They fell directly on the Bible. The air in the room grew tense. The minister stared at the moisture on his Bible, and then he grabbed up his coat and quickly left the cell. As he hurried down the hallway, Dave saw him and tried to speak to him. Reverend Blackburn brushed past him without so much as a word. The minister rushed from the prison and later refused to ever speak of the events of that night.

Everyone at the prison was tired of the rain boy. They had to keep him in a cell by himself, as no one wanted to be in a room with him. Many of the police officers and prison officials involved saw the water, which would roll up the wall and then launch itself across the room. There were often puddles of it in the room no matter what the prison officials did. The rain unnerved them, and more than one believed that it was paranormal in nature. They threatened Donnie, and he'd make them promises that he would stop it, but he never did.

Eventually Donnie was released. He floundered around for a while, but finally he began to heal. He took a job as a cook in a local restaurant, and the rain went away. To the people who witnessed the rain, Donnie was the biggest mystery of their lives. Some of the witnesses look back on the story with wonder, but others remember the fear they felt. No one is sure exactly what caused the strange rain to appear around Donnie, and they aren't really sure why his grandfather's death triggered the phenomenon.

Gettysburg

Ask people to name the most horrific battle of the Civil War, and they would likely say Gettysburg. Even the names given to many of the specific locations—Devil's Den, the Slaughter Pen, the Bloody Angle, the Valley of Death—reflected the fact that this was nothing short of hell on earth. Gettysburg was a field of bloodletting of unbelievable proportions, and today some say that acre for acre, it is the most haunted place in America.

Some say that the bloody battle that occurred there on July 1–3, 1863, was somehow foreordained to be fought in and around the small town located in south-central Pennsylvania. We know that neither commander wanted to bring on a battle at that site. The two giant armies accidentally brushed together there, and that touched off the massive slaughter of men on both sides. Were there otherworldly forces at work that would make the name Gettysburg hideously synonymous with the goriest fields of man's most frightening folly, war? Is there any other way to explain how thousands of men from across the limitless expanse of the country should all come to die together, virtually at once, at Gettysburg?

Many people wonder whether more paranormal activity occurs at Gettysburg on the anniversary of the battle than other times. It would seem so, but other factors must be considered as well. The town and battlefield are filled with visitors from out of town, including thousands of reenactors encamping for the counterfeit battle that occurs every anniversary. There are even more people in Gettysburg than usual, mainly because the battle was fought just before the Fourth of July. So perhaps it just seems more paranormal activity is occurring because more people are present to witness it. And could it be that reenactors attract ghostly activity? Perhaps the spirits feel more at home seeing people dressed the way they were the last time they strode this earth, cooking over campfires the way they did, eating the same kind of food, and suffering the same hardships.

The Ghost of General Washington

The very first ghost story of Gettysburg came from the soldiers themselves. It was the afternoon of July 1, 1863. The Union Army's V Corps had marched in from Maryland and was encamped just west of Hanover, Pennsylvania. No sooner had the men made camp than word came down that a great battle was taking place near a town a few miles to the west: Gettysburg. They began a march into the dusky night. It must have been an eerie sight in itself, the dark column undulating like a powerful serpent along the dusty road, lantern lights coming on in roadside farmhouses and reflecting off the burnished arms in a flickering dance.

Suddenly some of the men in the front of the column saw a figure swathed in white in the dark road ahead, beckoning and then turning to lead the army into the darkness. The column would catch up, men would pass a hand over their eyes to make sure what they saw was real, and a curious rumor began to pass back along the column. They recognized the figure, but it was impossible. The misty, mounted wraith wore a military uniform of a different era, a different war. He was cloaked in a long cape and had on a tricorn hat. It was, they were absolutely certain, General George Washington, leading the U.S. Army again, and the men took it as an omen that all would be well in the coming battle.

Major General Joshua Lawrence Chamberlain, who was marching in that column, was asked when he was an old man if he had heard that they were being led into battle by George Washington, then dead some sixty years. After pondering the question for a long time, he replied, "Yes, that report was circulated through our lines. . . . Doubtless it was a superstition." Reflecting further, as one who had seen all the horror and death of Gettysburg, as well as a score of other deadly battles, he added, "But yet, who among us can say that such a thing was impossible?"

The Soldier at Devil's Den

One young woman visiting Devil's Den heard a voice say to her in a soft Southern drawl, "What you're looking for is over there." She instinctively turned and almost immediately turned back . . . and the apparition who had spoken to her was gone, returned to where all good century-and-a-half-old soldiers go. Describing him to a park ranger, she drew a detailed picture of a man with shoulder-length hair, bare feet, ragged unkempt clothing, and a floppy hat—unknown to her, a description identical to the Texas troops whose blood washed over the boulders of Devil's Den as they captured it.

A month or so later, a photographer approached the desk at the park's visitor center and asked, "Are there any ghosts in Devil's Den?" As luck would have it, the same park ranger to whom the girl had told her story was at the desk and prompted the photographer to elaborate.

He explained how he had been in Devil's Den about a month before and was taking a picture of the massive rocks. When he developed his pictures, there, standing on one of the rocks, was a man who had not been there when he looked through the viewfinder. He had returned the next week to see if he could capture the anomaly again. This time he shot a whole roll of film. When he developed it, the left half of each picture was fine, but the right half—the half where the man had appeared before—was completely blurred in every frame. So now he was back to replicate the experiment. Asked to describe the man in the photo, he said he was ragged, with a floppy hat and shoulder-length hair, and appeared to be barefoot.

Spirits at the Slaughter Pen

Across Plum Run from Devil's Den is an area known as the Slaughter Pen, its name indicative of what transpired there. One night, a group of college students had parked their car in the lot near the Slaughter Pen and were wandering through Devil's Den. One had brought a Ouija board, which many paranormalists contend can open a spiritual door to some unwanted entities. They asked some questions of the board, which it apparently answered. One student finally asked whether the entities with which they were communicating would show themselves. The answer was yes.

Shocked, they packed up the board and began to nervously walk back to the car. Suddenly one of them stopped. "Look!" she said, pointing to the woods just beyond where the car was parked. "Do you see that?"

From the woods came an otherworldly bluish glow. As the students got closer to their car, some of them recognized the form of a man in a Civil War uniform accompanied by a woman in an old-fashioned hoop skirt. The spirits were moving toward the students' car.

For a moment it seemed like a race to see which—the living or the dead—would reach the car first. The students, now in a panic, fumbled with the keys and finally got into their car. As they turned on the headlights, the bluish forms vanished before them.

Phenomena at the Triangular Field

Another locale not far from Devil's Den is the Triangular Field. The name was given to the oddly shaped field by contemporary historians, so you will not find this place referred to in any of the soldiers' accounts of the fighting there. But the oddly shaped field had to have been burned into the memories of any soldier who survived the battle there.

A part of Smith's New York Battery held the top of Devil's Den, and their guns swept the Triangular Field. Several assaults by Hood's Texans failed to dislodge the guns or the Union infantry that backed them up. Then Benning's Georgians tried to take the field. Alongside the Texans, they were successful, but not without great cost. Benning's brigade had well over five hundred casualties, many of which occurred during the fight for the Triangular Field. One of the men killed in the fighting there became quite famous because of a photograph taken of him, a dead Confederate sharpshooter behind a rock barricade in Devil's Den. Sad as that photo is, it is even more horrible to behold once the details are explained. It seems that the poor soul was dragged to the spot and posed there by photographers who needed a dead body by that wall for dramatic effect. To give one's life for a cause is hard enough; to have one's mortal remains dragged about for a photographer's whim is beyond the bounds of humanity. Perhaps that is why people with cameras have so many problems in the Triangular Field.

Time and again, modern-day photographers will find their cameras without power after having fully charged their batteries. In the mid-1980s, the expensive, 35-millimeter cameras of three researchers all failed at the same time as they attempted to take pictures walking through the Triangular Field. Once they left the field, all the cameras began working again. Around the same time period, at least three high-quality television cameras failed while attempting to film in the field. When cameras do work there, strange forms of mist and globes of light will appear in the photos. Attempts at capturing electronic voice phenomena (EVP)—strange, eerie voices that are caught on tape but are not heard by the human ear—have been successful in that field. The voices on the tape have a military snap to them: "Yes, Sir," at least one has been heard to say.

Gettysburg's Child Ghosts

Perhaps the most disturbing kind of ghost stories are those about the spirits of children. Why must an innocent child, after suffering the loss of loving parents and enduring incarceration in an orphanage with a cruel headmistress, be made to abide here after death? This story comes down from many sources, and as with most folklore, bits and pieces have been added and taken away over the years, but the kernel of the story goes back to the aftermath of the battle.

As people were gathering the bodies, the stiffening corpse of a Union soldier was found hunched in a sitting position near the intersection of the railroad and Stratton Street. Clenched in his fingers was an ambrotype of three children. He had been struck just above the heart by a minié ball, the half-ounce, soft-lead, .58-caliber small-arms projectile of the era. The scene told a heart-rending story: Mortally wounded, he had dug in his haversack for the image, wanting to spend his last few seconds of life gazing at his children. Typical of the time when soldiers were not issued any government identity tags, he was buried near where he fell as an unknown soldier. The ambrotype was recovered by Dr. J. Francis Bournes, a volunteer surgeon with the Union Army from Philadelphia, along with the story of how it was found.

Dr. Bournes was wealthy, and he had the ambrotype copied and published in newspapers all over the country. You can imagine the horror when the man's former neighbor in Portville, New York, saw the images and showed them to Mrs. Amos Humiston. Gathering her children to her, Mrs. Humiston said the words that would be repeated hundreds of thousands of times over the four-year American Civil War: "Papa's never coming home again."

Sergeant Amos Humiston lies today in the New York section of the National Cemetery at Gettysburg. Because of the national publication of the ambrotype, money began to flood in, thanks to the sale of the image and a poetry-writing contest. Well-meaning individuals suggested that an orphanage be established in Gettysburg for the children of the war dead.

Mrs. Humiston was the first headmistress when the orphanage opened in 1866, and for a decade or so the children were happy. But then she remarried, and Mrs. Carmichael took over. As in a Dickens novel, the children's world turned upside down in a maelstrom of senselessly cruel punishments for meaningless infractions.

Screaming and crying were not uncommon sounds emanating from the orphanage and its outbuildings where children were sent as punishment on even the coldest days. Rumors flew: The new headmistress must be the cause. But every time inspectors were called to the orphanage, everything seemed in order. Until a few hours after they left, when it began all over again. Perhaps that's why, even to this day, visitors, employees, and even park rangers have heard the wails of children in and around the National Cemetery Lodge. A thorough search for children in trouble or being cruelly tortured invariably reveals nothing.

And perhaps the horror of the orphanage is the provenance of the story of how a young man came to be hidden in one of the rooms on the third floor of Stevens Hall on the Gettysburg College campus. Stevens Hall was not in existence during the Battle of Gettysburg, having been built between 1865 and 1868, so it serves as an example of how people must not jump to the conclusion that all the ghosts of Gettysburg can be traced back to the Civil War. In its earliest embodiment, Stevens served as a women's dormitory. From 1911 until 1935, it was used as an adjunct academy—a prep school—for Gettysburg College, housing students of precollege age. Today it is being used again as a dorm for female students.

But its first incarnation as a woman's dorm was the scene for the story of the children's spirits that continue to roam its halls, especially on the third floor. One night recently, a female student returned from a date. Her roommate was gone for the weekend, so when she opened the door to her room, she was surprised to see a young woman standing before a full-length mirror, admiring herself. The student cried out in surprise, "Who are you? What are you doing here?" The young female stranger did not answer but appeared to run into the closet next to the mirror. The student walked to the closet and turned on the light but could see no one. She began to slide blouses around and moved boxes, but to no avail. The young woman had vanished.

If this were the only case, it could be dismissed as merely the overactive imagination of a postadolescent woman who had stayed up too late. But another night, another young woman entered her locked room rather late. There, to her astonishment, was a young girl standing in front of her mirror, holding clothes from the closet up to her slim frame as if attempting to decide what to try on next. The student shouted, and the stranger ducked into the nearby closet. Rummaging through the closet brought this student no closer to solving the mystery: The young girl again had disappeared.

But perhaps the most disturbing event, because of the regularity with which it occurs, involves a young boy who was housed—or hidden, some say—on the third floor of Stevens Hall one cold Gettysburg winter. Where the boy came from can only be guessed, although with the orphanage with its cruel headmistress just across town, and some kindhearted young ladies living in a cozy dormitory, it can readily be surmised.

Everything seemed okay for a while, at least. The students would sneak him food from their dinners and bring him simple toys to keep him occupied while they studied. His life was good, until one particular bitterly cold night when the matron of Stevens Hall came knocking on the young ladies' door. The earliest of the dorm rooms had no closets—those were a later addition. Fearing that the matron would look underneath the beds, there was only one place the young women's panicked minds could think of to hide the boy: outside the window.

They helped the young boy out onto the window ledge, begging him to hang on a few seconds until they got rid of the matron. They closed the curtains and opened the door. The matron made a cursory search of the room, then ordered the young students downstairs to endure a more thorough interrogation. More than once during the hourlong questioning, they thought of their young friend perched on that frigid windowsill, suffering through the weird, chilling winds that swept off the darkened battlefields just to the north.

Finally they were dismissed from the matron's cozy apartment and virtually sprinted the three floors to their room. They threw open the window to rescue . . . no one. The boy had vanished. They ran outside, but there was no trace of him. No tracks in the snow, no impression where he had fallen, and thankfully—but mysteriously—no body.

But something sinister must have happened that night, because although the boy is gone, he is not quite *all* gone. A modern-day student was sitting at her desk studying in her third-floor Stevens Hall room when, out of the corner of her eye, she saw something at her window. She pulled her eyes away from her textbook, and as they adjusted to the light, she saw the inexplicable: a child's face hovering outside the third-floor window, peering in at her. The odd thing was that the little boy's face was blue—that strange, otherworldly cast taken on by human skin after it has been exposed too long to the cold. Shocked and frightened by a face levitating in a window three stories up, she stood, and the blue, boyish face vanished.

This might be dismissed entirely, explained away as the effects of too much study and an overwrought imagination, except for the fact that this student was not the only one to have seen him. In fact, he's been seen so many times over the years at the third-floor window of Stevens Hall that the women who live there have named him the Blue Boy.

Perhaps the most eerie happening occurred within the last few years. It was another cold winter night in Gettysburg—so cold, in fact, that frost had etched its crystalline haze across the third-floor windows of Stevens Hall. Again, a young female student was at her desk studying when her eye was caught by a boyish blue face floating outside her window. No sooner did she focus her eyes on it than it went away, floating to one side of the window.

Startled and unable to come up with a reasonable explanation, she shook her head, rubbed her eyes, and went back to her books. Again, as if in need, the cold, blue visage drifted from the side of the window to center itself in the frosty pane and stare beseechingly at her.

That was it. Twice was too much. She stood and left her warm room to get a soft drink and calm herself. After taking a few deep breaths in front of the soda machine, she convinced herself that the vision was just an illusion caused by too many late hours studying. She returned, a calmer woman, to her room.

Once back in the room, she looked cautiously at the window. She was relieved to see that no blue, childlike face stared back at her. But then, in the frosty coating on the outside of the window, she saw scratched in a pleading, childish scrawl, the backward words "Help me."

Open Portal at Little Round Top

At Gettysburg, portals into another world may explain claims of the visualization and sudden dematerialization of objects, people, and scenes from the past. An apport refers to a physical item that is passed between worlds, as well as the act of an object moving from one dimension into another. An instance of a portal opening is believed to have happened one hot, sultry day on Little Round Top.

It was July 2, 1981, the anniversary of the battle. For years, a private company has sponsored a reenactment of the Battle of Gettysburg. For safety's sake, reenactors are allowed to carry only blank rounds—black powder rolled up in paper, looking like the real thing of more than a century past, but minus the lead minié balls that were wrapped inside the originals. If a reenactor is found with live ammunition, the offender will be required to appear in federal court and pay a substantial fine. Needless to say, no serious reenactor ever carries live ammunition.

After the mock battle that July day, two reenactors were relaxing and enjoying the sunset from the magnificent vantage point of Little Round Top, attempting to envision the setting before them as it was exactly 118 years before, to the minute. Their historians' minds would have been filled with horrid images of the maelstrom of battle. Where they sat on Little Round Top, the events had been especially gruesome. Many of the rock walls the defensive line of the Union Army's V Corps had built for protection are still there. Perhaps they were imagining the hundreds of troops surging back and forth, up and down the western slope of the hill.

As they gazed downslope into what was later named the Valley of Death, they may have envisaged bloody heaps of bodies where the units stood and fought and brave men fell. They could see the reflection of the sun glistening in a small stream rechristened by the soldiers, Bloody Run because, for a few desperate hours in American history, it ran red with the blood of the men who fought across its banks. They might have recalled from their reading one Confederate officer's comment that there, where they sat, had been puddles of blood in some places on the rocks.

From the tangled brush just down the hill from where they sat, the reenactors heard a rustling and saw what they took to be a fellow Federal reenactor emerge from the bushes and begin climbing wearily toward them. As he approached, the two were astounded at his authenticity. His face was stained with sweat, his beard fouled with the black grime that comes from biting the ends off paper cartridges to expose the black powder necessary for loading Civil War–era weapons. "Hello, fellows." His voice rang with a Yankee twang. "Mighty hot fight there today, weren't it?" The two reenactors were about to compliment him on his realistic appearance, but before they could, he reached into his cartridge box and pulled out two rounds of ammunition. "Here," he said. "Take these. You boys may need 'em tomorrow." He gave them an odd look, turned, and began walking back down the hill toward the rock walls that were once the defensive lines, fought over and bled upon by soldiers dressed just like him.

The two reenactors watched for just a second as the soldier made his way into the dusk. Rolling the cartridges over in their hands, the two reenactors realized that these were not blank, hand-made reenactment cartridges. They were exact replicas of Civil War–era ammunition, tied and folded correctly, with beeswax coating to waterproof them. In fact, they looked as if they had come out of a museum. The reenactors could feel the minié ball inside of each one. They looked down the slope to where the soldier had retreated just a second or two before, but he had vanished into the evening mist, which at Gettysburg often seems to take the shape of long lines of infantry ready for battle.

After the incident, one of the two reenactors took the rounds home and placed them in a special case. But in spite of the care, within a month the paper, wax, and string had all disintegrated into dust—everything but the lead minié balls. It seemed as if time had caught up with the relics at last.

The Haunting of Gettysburg College

Founded in 1832, Gettysburg College was known as Pennsylvania College during its early years. The board of trustees changed its name some time after the battle to take advantage of the area's notorious fame. At the time of the battle, the college consisted of three buildings: the President's House, Pennsylvania Hall, and Linnean Hall. Pennsylvania Hall was also called "Old Dorm," since it was used as both classroom and dormitory. During the battle, this building, which was one of the largest in the area, was commandeered as a makeshift hospital, first by the Federal surgeons, behind whose lines the building stood on the morning of July 1, and then by the Confederate surgeons, behind whose lines it stood after the Confederate victory on the afternoon of July 1. So the building contained both Union and Confederate wounded.

While the battle raged around it, Old Dorm would have been a scene of almost unimaginable suffering and horror. Usually the upper floors of such wartime hospitals were reserved for the recovery rooms. The true horror was saved for the lower floor, which in most cases became the operating room. If a soldier was struck in an extremity by a minié ball, the common small-arms projectile of the time, the soft lead bullet flattened against the bone and shattered it into dozens of shards. Amputation was a certainty, and many surgeons prided themselves on how quickly they could amputate a young man's arm or leg. The operation was most likely done without anesthesia, and quick cutting meant less time in profound pain. After its separation from the owner, the limb was tossed unceremoniously out the nearest window. Reports of pyramids of feet, hands, legs, and arms up to the windowsills were common.

If soldiers were struck in the body, the surgeons, to whom internal surgery was almost unknown and certainly too time-consuming when hundreds of other patients were waiting, would let them lie. That perhaps was the best thing they could have done, for Pasteur's and Lister's work in antiseptics lay a decade ahead. Army surgeons did not sterilize instruments between operations. They barely had time to rinse the slippery gore off their hands in a bloody bucket of water before the next patient was brought to the table. Often, after minor medical exploration of a scratch, a patient would initially appear to be recovering but then, two weeks later, suddenly take a turn for the worse and die within hours, a victim of blood poisoning, unwittingly introduced by a surgeon who had explored an abdominal cavity moments before he looked at the scratch.

Every hospital had a roped-in area nearby for those struck in the head but, incredibly, not killed by the hot lead. While some lay quivering in the dewy grass, others wandered, blankly staring, their mindless bodies still obeying the last marching orders from this world. When they hit the ropes, they would turn to march off toward yet another unknown foe.

Confederate commander Robert E. Lee used the cupola of Old Dorm to watch the fighting, which may explain the modern-day sightings of a spirit that has come to be called the Sentry in the structure high above the campus. An unsuspecting student usually first hears a sound—like the snapping of arms to attention, some say. When the student looks up, there in the cupola, which is eternally locked for security reasons, is what appears to be a man dressed in the garb of a Civil War soldier. He paces to one side of the cupola, does a sharp about-face, and then returns to the other side—still guarding, fourteen decades later, the commander of the Army of Northern Virginia.

And if the testimony of two college administrators and the head of security is to be believed, there has been evidence of even more impressive devotion to duty. All three were working late one night, the administrators on the fourth floor of Pennsylvania Hall and the security guard in his office just a building away. It was time to head for home, and the two women walked through the darkened halls of Old Dorm to the elevator. They punched the button for the first floor, the doors closed, and the elevator began to descend, but it continued past the first floor and into the basement. Thinking that there had been a mechanical malfunction, they punched the button to go back up to the first floor. But instead of the elevator rising, the doors opened to reveal a scene out of time and logic.

There before them was the scene of a century past, with blood-stained doctors and orderlies performing the horrid tasks of slicing through flesh and muscle, sawing through human bone, and sewing artery and skin flaps, all the while attempting to hold down a struggling patient. Off in the blood-moistened corners were other injured soldiers, some waiting for their turn on the table, others groggy from their pain recently endured.

The two women punched at the buttons frantically, but the doors would not close. Then, from around the doors of the elevator, came a young orderly. He was so close the women could see the pleading look in his eyes, which they felt seemed to say, "Either come into this man-made hell and help, or let me enter with you and take me away from here!" As he took a step toward them, the doors finally began to close slowly, and the elevator started to rise.

The women ran from the building straight to the security office to report what they saw. Believing it was a fraternity prank, the guard was eager to catch the students in the act. They got to Old Dorm and entered within just a couple minutes of the women's hasty departure. Certainly, the guard thought, there was no way the fraternity could clean up the kind of mess the women had described that quickly. Bravely, the women got back on the elevator and descended into the basement.

The doors opened to reveal . . . nothing. The pristine storage area was immaculate. There were no stains, no bodies, no doctors, and no orderly begging to be released from his eternal prison.

The administrators have since moved on to other institutions of higher learning. While at Gettysburg, however, they sometimes still worked late into the night. But if it was after dark when they left the building that had once echoed with the screams of tortured soldiers, they always chose to use the stairs.

Roughed Up by a Gettysburg Ghost

Nearly all reported ghost sightings or encounters appear to be harmless in nature, merely creating curiosity or mild confusion and barely scaring the percipient. Though physical attacks by ghosts on live humans seem to be extremely rare, one such incident has been reported at Gettysburg.

A woman was visiting Gettysburg in the fall of 1999 with her husband and brother. The trio had been touring the battlefield and ate a picnic lunch. They had visited Little Round Top and Devil's Den, and as the wife had an appointment later that day, they determined they had time for just one more stop. They chose the infamous Wheatfield.

During the late-afternoon hours of July 2, 1863, as part of a massive Confederate sweep toward the Union lines on Cemetery Ridge,

Georgia soldiers had run into Union troops on the southern edge of farmer Rose's wheat field. More units poured into the twenty-six-acre field as Federal troops attempted to save their endangered comrades, only to be overwhelmed as more Confederate reinforcements arrived to help the other side.

Over the course of a few short hours, the Wheatfield was covered with the torn and wrecked bodies of the dead and wounded. The fighting was savage, with some units fighting so close that officers were able to use their pistols on the enemy, and more that one commander ordered, "Fix bayonets," in preparation for hand-to-hand combat. Captures were wholesale, and soldiers were physically manhandled and sent back roughly to the rear if they would not go peacefully. In fierce battles, particularly at Fredericksburg before Gettysburg, the wounded often grabbed at comrades going into the battle in a futile effort to save their lives from certain destruction.

The trio visiting the Wheatfield in 1999 wanted to get a few photos. The woman's brother, a photography buff, exited the vehicle with his expensive, professional-grade camera, but it suddenly froze. The shutter just seemed to hang up. The strange thing was that when he turned toward the South Mountain range, away from the Wheatfield, the camera worked perfectly, but when he turned back toward the field once covered with the bodies of the slain, the camera again refused to function.

The woman's husband picked up her 35-millimeter camera from the car. The camera had shot four rolls of film already that day, and only four pictures had been taken on the roll inside the camera, which had always functioned properly. Halfway into the Wheatfield, the husband stopped to take a shot. Suddenly the camera's rewind mechanism whirred into activity. Thinking that perhaps he had inadvertently pressed the wrong button, he examined the camera. It had only rewound to the first photo on the roll and did not rewind the entire film back into the canister.

The woman's brother, bothered by the fact that he could not get a single picture of the Wheatfield and that time was running short, strode back to their van. "I'm telling you," he said, "there's something about that field. I can't get a decent shot of it."

The husband grabbed the party's third camera—a foolproof little 110. "I'll get you a picture of that field," he said angrily, stomping off across the golden Wheatfield. This camera worked just fine, and he snapped a few pictures.

Back in the van, as the three of them were driving to the woman's appointment, her husband began complaining about a sharp pain under his arm. He took off his heavy shirt, and there under his arm was a long, bright red welt. He mentally retraced his steps during the last hour, but he could think of no explanation for the appearance of the mark.

They returned home later that night and were preparing for bed. After his bath, the husband came out into the living room. He had an odd look on his face and was having trouble formulating his question. Finally he asked, "Did you ever hear of the ghosts in Gettysburg hurting anyone?"

From the tone of his voice, his wife knew he was upset. "Why?" she asked.

"When I got my bath tonight, I found this." He lifted the sleeve of his T-shirt. There on the underside of his arm was a large bruise in the exact shape of a handprint, positioned such that it would have been impossible to be self-inflicted. It was at approximately the same area where the welt had been earlier. The woman took pictures of the bruise, and indeed they look as if phantom fingers had grabbed her husband's arm with enough force to burst the small blood vessels below the skin at the tip of each finger. In the photo, the mark is reminiscent of the bruises a wrestler sometimes gets when an opponent grabs him by the arm.

A day or two later, the woman was talking on the phone with her brother and told him about the strange bruise on her husband's arm—received, apparently, from some unseen entity in the historic Wheatfield at Gettysburg. Her brother was shocked. "You're kidding, right?"

The woman assured him she wasn't. But his reaction made her ask him if something was wrong. He hesitated and tried to change the subject, but the woman pressed him. Finally he admitted that he, too, had been the victim of some unknown and unseen malevolence in the Wheatfield. "The other night when I was getting into the bath, I noticed, about four inches down from my knee on the left calf, a big bruise that looked like someone grabbed me there. I don't bruise easily, and I can't imagine how it got there. It's just a big handprint as if someone grabbed me really hard and dug in."

Penn State

THOSE WHO STUDY PARANORMAL PHENOMENA GENERALLY BELIEVE THAT the presence of young people enhances supernatural activities. Reports of poltergeist activity can almost always be linked to adolescents—usually young women, but often young men as well—and the activity can be quite dramatic. Physical items being thrown around the room, balls of light flying by, and doors and windows slamming all seem to take place most often around young people.

Many blame such phenomena on the mental energy of the adolescent rather than on ghosts. Others subscribe to the theory that spirits need energy to manifest, as evidenced when batteries are drained in their presence, and therefore are more active when there is more energy to draw from. And who has more energy than young people?

Colleges certainly are filled with the unbridled energy of the young. So perhaps it is no wonder that Pennsylvania State University—Penn State for short—has its share of stories of unexplainable, mystifying ghostly activity.

Old Coaly, the Ghostly Mule

It seems that Penn State's Main Campus at State College is home to several ghostly entities. The oldest is that of Old Coaly, a mule that helped haul the stone for the original buildings in the 1850s. The little mule died of old age after the school was built, and the university obtained his body. Old Coaly became part of a display in Old Main Building.

After the turn of the twentieth century, the campus caught fire. Among the items saved from the flames was the carcass of Old Coaly, which was placed in storage in the basement of Watts Hall. Soon after that, both staff and students began to report sightings of a mule standing outside the storage room door. Other folks reported braying sounds. In the college atmosphere, the staff began to suspect that a student was playing jokes; however, no one was ever caught playing a joke or confessed to such a prank. It seemed that Old Coaly wanted more attention than he was getting in the basement of Watts Hall.

In the 1960s, Old Coaly finally got a new home in the Agricultural Building. He became part of a display there, but apparently he is still not happy with his accommodations—Old Coaly has been reported to haunt that building as well. Staff and students for many years have claimed to have seen the little mule or heard his braying at odd moments.

The Spirits of Schwab Auditorium

No one has ever been better known on the Penn State campus than Charles Schwab. Schwab made his fortune in the steel industry, and like many wealthy men of his time, he believed that it was his duty to be philanthropic. He and his wife donated $155,000 to build a new 972-seat auditorium at the university. Schwab took a great interest in the school and was a member of its board of trustees for more than thirty years. He saw his gift built, and some say that Schwab is still visiting the auditorium named in his honor.

Staff and students have several tales to tell about Schwab Auditorium. They believe it is actually haunted by more than one entity. According to published reports, people have heard footsteps, seen a figure walking by, and felt someone tugging at them as if to get their attention while working onstage.

A ghostly presence is said to watch the stage from the balcony. Actors have claimed that a male figure was watching them as they rehearsed. At times, staff members have witnessed a spring-loaded seat in the auditorium spontaneously going down as if someone were sitting in it . . . but no one can be seen in the seat. Just as mysteriously as the seat went down, it would eventually go back up. It is believed that the entity who watches the actors so keenly is the ghost of Charles Schwab, still taking an interest in his theater.

According to a maintenance man who works in the auditorium, one of the specters there enjoys playing pranks. Staff members have reported objects disappearing and reappearing in the theater. More than one have laid down tools they were working with, only to discover seconds later that tools were gone—despite the fact that they were alone. Usually the item has turned up in some obvious place where the person had already searched for it.

A mysterious male stranger who has long hair and appears to be quite real has been seen on the stage. One unlucky employee encountered this phantom one night on the stage and initially mistook the fellow for a female production manager. When he realized it was not who he had thought, he hurried toward the stage to confront the man. As he drew close, the man seemed to glide toward stage right. Much to the employee's surprise, the phantom did not stop at the proscenium wall, but passed through it and was gone. The startled employee took a few minutes to recover before leaving the building that evening.

The director of performing arts in the early 1970s had his own encounter with a spectral being in the auditorium. One evening, the director was working late when he realized that a misty entity was forming right beside him. The man froze for a few seconds, as the figure continued to materialize. To his utter amazement, the director soon was looking at a tall man formed in shades of gray, with long hair and a tattered Revolutionary War style jacket. The director could see him clearly for several seconds.

Despite his encounter, the director tried to convince himself that he was mistaken about what he had seen. However, he could not deny his second encounter. On that day, the director came face-to-face with the same man in the basement of the building. The long-haired spirit stared right at the director, and their eyes met. He was certain that the ghost saw him too.

No one has ever adequately explained who the man was or why he haunts the building, but there seems little doubt that a Revolutionary War–era ghost is sharing space in the grand auditorium with the less aged entities. It seems that they must have built Penn State's Main Campus on haunted ground.

Another ghost who is thought to haunt Schwab Auditorium is that of the university's seventh president, George Atherton. Atherton's grave can be found just outside the north wall of the building, and since his death, people have claimed to have seen and heard him in the auditorium.

George's wife, Frances, also is believed to haunt the main campus. People have reportedly seen her looking out of the Old Botany Building's attic windows that face the Schwab Auditorium. Some people say she is unhappy that the school placed Pollock Street between the two buildings and has come back to show her opposition. Others say, however, that she is there to gaze out on Schwab Auditorium in hopes of seeing her husband.

The Spirit in the Stacks

Yet another ghost is said to haunt Penn State's Main Campus, this one tragic and sad. At about 5 P.M. on November 28, 1969, Betsy Aardsma, a twenty-two-year old graduate student, let out a long, shrill scream while she was studying in the university's Pattee Library. The young woman was up in "the Stacks," a remote, dark area on the second floor. Others hurried to Betsy's aid, but the pretty young woman had been mortally stabbed through the heart and lay dying. Betsy was taken to the Ritenour Health Center, where she soon was pronounced dead.

Despite their best efforts, the police never solved the case of the murdered coed. No clues were forthcoming. Betsy never named her killer, and to this day the person who took her life remains free. The police interviewed more than 650 people, but no one ever gave them a lead that broke the case.

The tragic death of a young woman taken far too early is bound to spawn a few ghostly tales, and soon after her death, people began to whisper that Betsy was now haunting the library. People reported hearing a single scream from the Stacks where Betsy was attacked. Others claimed to see a pretty young woman with dark hair, who seemed to be looking at the books until she suddenly just disappeared.

Employees and patrons of Pattee Library will tell you that the Stacks have changed little since Betsy's death. No new lighting or security has been added. Over the years, the excitement over Betsy's death has died down. But occasionally a very frightened student will hurry to the library desk to ask about the young woman in the Stacks or report that someone has just screamed up there. The librarian duly checks the area, and then explains to the frightened student that it's probably just Betsy's ghost—waiting there, perhaps forever, since her murderer was never found.

Phantoms at Wiestling Hall

Penn State has several satellite campuses, many of which boast their own spooks and specters. At the Mont Alto campus, Wiestling Hall has long been associated with two different ghosts.

Colonel George Wiestling contracted malaria while serving in the Union forces during the Civil War. He was sent home to recuperate, and he decided to run an iron furnace in Mont Alto, where he had financial interests, while he recovered. Colonel Wiestling took over the iron furnace and began a series of reformations. He instituted a six-day workweek, which allowed men to spend a day with their families. At the time, this was a very progressive idea. Wiestling believed strongly that if he gave his men Sunday off, he would have better workers for the rest of the week.

In 1864, Wiestling officially took over the large cabin that was home to the ironmaster. Over the years, the iron furnace and cabin saw a lot more changes thanks to the Colonel. When he moved his two sisters and his brother into the cabin with him, he found that he needed more room, so he remodeled and built onto the building. By the time he was done, he had built a large and lovely home.

In 1893, the property was taken over by the state of Pennsylvania, and a school of forestry management was set up on the grounds. By then, Colonel Wiestling and his brother were both dead, but his sisters were allowed to remain in the building. The ladies stayed on at Wiestling Hall for some time, but eventually they were forced to move from their longtime home.

Wiestling Hall eventually became a food service hall and dormitory. The staff and students have often reported that Colonel Wiestling is haunting the building he put so much effort into during his lifetime. Reports of footsteps in empty rooms, pans and dishes clattering together when no one has touched them, and little pranks and jokes being played are common. On occasion, however, the Colonel has been known to go a bit further. Food service workers in the kitchen have reported hearing footsteps walking around behind them, as if someone were checking on their work. They saw and heard dishes moving across countertops, and pots seemingly picked themselves up off of shelves and landed on nearby tables. Equipment has been known to turn itself on, and the staff insists that Colonel Wiestling is still looking after things.

One food service worker staying in the building in the 1960s reported that he witnessed unnerving phenomena. The man claimed that on several occasions, he'd heard banging on locked doors. Suddenly the locked door would swing open, even though no one was near it. When the door was examined, the locking mechanism was still in the locked position. This happened to not just one door, but to virtually any door locked at Wiestling Hall during that time period.

By far the most shocking evidence that Colonel Wiestling is still in the building came when a student took a photograph of Wiestling Hall. The student was amazed to discover that a man posing before the building in the snapshot looked exactly like existing photographs of Colonel Wiestling. Apparently the Colonel enjoys having his picture taken, too.

It seems that the other ghostly presence in Wiestling Hall is not there by choice. Thirty-year-old Sadie Hurley was working in the building when a great tragedy made her part of its history. One morning in May 1911, Sadie's former boyfriend, William Reed, came to Wiestling Hall very upset. He accused her of having some photographs and papers of his from the Spanish-American War and demanded that Sadie return them. At first she protested that she did not have his papers, but when she saw how agitated he was, she said she'd go fetch them.

People in the building that morning later stated that Sadie was agitated and upset and took a long time to return to the dining hall. When she came back, she told William she could not find the papers. She tried to calm him and insisted that she'd look for them again if only he'd leave so she could get her work done.

William was furious, so Sadie hurried back upstairs on the pretext of looking for the materials again. Eventually she was forced to return and again tell him she did not have the papers he sought.

William suddenly pulled a revolver from his clothing and shot Sadie. The wounded girl ran for her life, fleeing from the back porch into the kitchen with William in pursuit. He shot her again, and she ran farther into the building. In the dining hall, Sadie was cornered, and William shot her directly through the heart. He then turned and left the building, seeming unconcerned about what had just transpired.

As soon as William left, people came to Sadie's aid. They carried her upstairs to her attic bedroom while someone else ran for the doctor. She lived long enough to be placed on her bed in the little attic room. One of the matrons at the school, Miss Sarah Conklin, accompanied Sadie to her room and comforted the poor woman in the brief moments before her death. Sadie died while Sarah held her.

William Reed was arrested for the cold-blooded murder, but he insisted that he had never meant to shoot Sadie. He claimed that he could not remember doing so. He told the police he had brought the gun to the school only to frighten Sadie into giving back his papers. However, William was tried and convicted for the murder of Sadie Hurley and was hanged in the Franklin County prison yard. The execution of William Reed was the last execution in Franklin County history.

Sadie, however, seems not to have left Wiestling Hall. People have long reported hearing phantom footsteps hurrying into what was once Sadie's room. Once two college boys decided to stake out the room in hopes of confronting the phantom. They chose the night of her death and sat in the darkness. They had flashlights and felt that they were perfectly safe.

For hours the young men waited, and then at last they heard the hurried footsteps coming up the stairs. The steps came closer and turned into the area where Sadie's room had been. The boys grabbed their flashlights to make sure it wasn't just pranksters, but both flashlights refused to work. Suddenly the footsteps stopped and turned, and then the person hurried back down the stairs. As soon as the footsteps left the room, the flashlights came on. The boys could see that no one was in the room, the attic, or on the stairs, but they could still hear the footsteps retreating down the stairs.

Students staying in the dormitory rooms at Wiestling Hall have also reported strange events such as furniture moving by itself, electronic devices turning themselves on, and doors locking and unlocking themselves at will. The students have also been treated to visits by the sounds of phantom footsteps.

Perhaps the strangest manifestation at Wiestling Hall is the blood said to be found on the attic stairs. Over the years, several people have reported that they heard hurried footsteps going up the attic stairs, and when they went to check on the sounds, they found a blood trail leading up the steps and into one of the old staff bedrooms.

The Ghost Buck

Penn State's McKeesport campus has a lovely ghost that the staff and students there have treasured for years. The campus has a grove of trees where deer have long lived. Among the herd was a buck that had been there for some time. He was a massive creature and regal in nature. Anyone who saw him knew that he was special, and he could not be mistaken for any of the lesser animals because this deer sported a sixteen-point rack of horns. The students nicknamed the beast Duke, and he became something of an unofficial mascot.

For about fifteen years, Duke ruled the campus. He came and went as he pleased, and folks made way for Duke, but eventually he died. There was no mistaking the body when it was found, because the dead deer had that regal sixteen-point set of antlers.

But the staff and students claim that Duke still reigns on the McKeesport campus. There have been many reports through the years of a massive buck with a sixteen-point rack of horns seen roaming the campus. Those who remember Duke just smile fondly and nod. They are glad that Duke never really left them.

The Lady in White

The most tragic ghost among the Penn State spooks would have to be that of a young woman seen at Penn State's Beaver campus. The old administration building of this campus was originally built by the state as a tuberculosis sanatorium. At one time, the disease ravaged the nation. Pennsylvania had so many cases of tuberculosis that each county had its own sanatorium to care for the victims.

With the advent of a vaccine, the disease was eradicated, and the old sanatoriums were turned over to other uses. The building in Beaver became office space. Through the years, it was rumored to be haunted. People talked about phantom footsteps in the halls. Staff in the building told stories about phantom footsteps coming into their offices. One employee insisted that when he worked late, he would hear a man walk into his office but never saw anyone. Others claimed that they saw a matronly nurse walking her ward at night. But most people said that the Lady in White haunted the building.

In 1994, a nurse named Barbara came to work at the school, and that would bring the haunting to a new level. The nurse did not believe in ghosts and was not interested in supernatural tales when she first arrived. A former missionary, she simply did not accept that a haunting could even occur. But the old administration building and the Lady in White were about to change her life forever.

The nurse had been working in the building several months without incident and was not concerned about ghosts the day of her first encounter. It was early in the evening, and the nurse was hurrying to finish up so that she could go home. She needed to get some forms copied before she could leave, so she hurried to the copy room. Along the way, she passed the faculty lounge. The room had large, glass windows that overlooked the campus. Standing and gazing out the windows was a young woman. The nurse did a double take because she had thought she was alone in the building. She immediately realized that she was not watching a living person. The figure she saw was a slight young woman with long, blond hair that fell loosely down her back. The young woman wore a long, white nightgown or dress.

A sudden feeling of great sadness came over the nurse. She could feel this woman's sorrow and sense her thoughts. The young woman was mourning the fact that she'd never have a real life. She was struggling with the fact that she was about to die. The Lady in White was grieving for the loss of her dreams. She'd never get married, have children, grow old, or do any of the other things she had dreamed of. It was such a great loss that it was terribly hard for her to accept.

As these thoughts and feelings flooded the nurse, she suddenly realized that the Lady in White was aware that she was being watched. The ghostly girl began to turn. The nurse broke her paralysis and hurried down the hall. She was terrified that the young woman would ask her for help and even more frightened that she'd have to explain that she could not help her.

For weeks, the nurse kept this encounter to herself. No one else had ever spoken about such a personal experience with the Lady in White. Others had glimpsed her, felt her, or thought someone was there, but no one had seen her and experienced her thoughts and feelings as the nurse had. The nurse began to listen more closely when the subject of ghosts came up, but no one else ever talked of experiencing the entity in such an intimate way.

For three months, the nurse kept her own counsel about the ghost she had seen. One day she was in her office working, when suddenly she heard a voice coming from the wall where the medicine chest was. A young adult woman called out "Nurse Barbara" twice. The nurse whirled around, but no one was there. She was staring at an empty wall. Just as she turned back, she heard the voice once again calling to her clearly.

The nurse got up and opened the medicine cabinet. She examined it, but there was nothing in it that could have been used to broadcast a voice. Next she examined the hallway and the rooms nearby. No one was there.

The nurse began to suspect that the Lady in White was seeking her out because she was a nurse. In the last days of the young woman's life, she surely had been comforted and cared for by the nurses of her time. Perhaps she was reaching out to her thinking that as a nurse, she also would care.

The nurse could no longer keep her experiences to herself. She approached a couple fellow workers whom she trusted and told them of her experiences. Eventually her story leaked out, and the nurse actually appeared on television and told of her ghostly experiences. But she paid a great price for telling her story. Some of the people in her town and her church family were very upset at her for giving credence to the ghostly tales.

The nurse had one more encounter in the old administration building with a phantom she believed was the Lady in White. It was a cold winter day, and the nurse hurried inside the building by way of a back door that she did not usually use. As she neared the door, she felt drawn to look down at the basement window. What she saw there made her stop: Two eyes were looking out at her. She saw no face, no body—only two eyes, and they gazed directly at her. In a rush of feeling, the nurse understood that this was the Lady in White and that she stood there often to be out of the way and watch the world pass by. Later the nurse learned that the bodies of the tuberculosis victims were taken first to the basement of this building, and then from there to another building nearby.

After hearing the nurse's stories, one of the men in the administration department set out to learn more. He found two different people who had known the building when it was used as a sanatorium. One was an old man, who told the administrator that he had lived on the grounds as a child because his father worked there. He said he had seen the Lady in White many times while she was alive as he was growing up on the property.

The second person was an elderly lady who also had grown up in the area. She claimed that she knew the identity of the Lady in White. As a little girl, she said, she had frequently played on the grounds and sometimes talked to a young woman with long, blond hair who was there for treatment and often walked around wearing a white nightgown and robe. The young woman was only in her late teens and was terribly lonely. She soon died, and it was only after her death that the ghost stories started. One night the little girl sneaked onto the grounds and saw the ghost herself. She was not frightened, however, because she recognized the spirit as that of her former friend.

Altoona and Central Pennsylvania

The Central Pennsylvania area is dotted by rural communities and farmlands. In the center of the rustic area is Altoona, a once fine city that today is only a reminder of what it used to be. The railroad built Altoona, fueled the migration of many nationalities to the area, and gave the region its spice. Today the city still hosts trains, and nearby is the world-famous Horseshoe Curve.

Along with the people came their beliefs, superstitions, and ghosts. The real wealth of Central Pennsylvania is in the people, whose work ethic, faith, and cultures have enriched the landscape. The people who came to the area worked hard to build the railroad, but they never forgot their own independence. Those traits are still seen today in the people of the region.

Phantoms in the Railroaders Museum

In the mid-1800s, Altoona was the railroad capital of the world. It was a utilitarian town dedicated to building, repairing, and keeping trains moving. What it lacked in aesthetic beauty, it made up for by the hard work of the people who came from around the world for the opportunity to begin a new life working in the railroad shops. Slovaks, Czechs, Poles, Germans, Jews, Italians, and many more came for the work. Fortunes were made and a nation was built on the backs of those hardworking men and women. The Altoona Railroaders Memorial Museum is dedicated to them. It's not a museum about railroading, but about railroaders.

The museum is located in what was once the Master Mechanics building for the Pennsylvania Railroad (PRR). Built in 1882, it served many different purposes through the years: office space, the PRR Infirmary, a warehouse, a doctor's office, the PRR Test Lab, the Master Mechanics building, and others. It has been gutted down to the outside brickwork and refurbished with a modern computer and electrical system. The building now houses many artifacts from railroading history, and displays portray various phases of railroading life.

Even before the building opened, paranormal activity seemed to be occurring. The first museum director was training some volunteers to help during the museum's opening. As he sat in the back of training room on the third floor listening to some folks talking, he noticed two men coming up the hallway. The men were dressed in work pants and flannel shirts, and they seemed to hesitate near the door to the training room. The curator thought perhaps the men were volunteers who had come in late and didn't want to interrupt the meeting. He slipped quietly out of the room to welcome the two men, but by the time he got to the hallway, they had turned and were going back in the opposite direction toward the display about the PRR Test Lab. The curator called after the men but suddenly realized there was something very wrong about them: He could see right through them. The men took a couple more steps, and then faded from sight.

That was the first confirmed sighting of spirits in the Altoona Railroaders Museum. The curator chose not to mention his observations to anyone, however. He didn't want to be the man who brought up the subject of ghosts.

For several years, the museum staff did not talk about the ghosts, but others seemed to have experiences as well. One of the male security guards who opened up in the morning often heard footsteps on the second-floor area above the entrance called the Bridge. No one was ever seen or tripped the alarms, but the people opening up or closing often reported hearing the phantom footsteps running along.

The many displays sometimes turned themselves on and off, although they were shut off at the main switch. Piles of stuffed toys would be found in the aisles of the gift shop when it was opened up, as well as books stacked in the walkways. Eventually the woman who ran the gift shop made a point of being the one to close and open up in order to be sure that someone was not playing a practical joke, but she continued to find the toys and books out of place.

The first curator had two more sightings in the building. He was working in the Test Lab one day when he heard footsteps coming toward him. He looked up to see a man in a white lab coat hurry by. The man turned and went into the wall. On another occasion, the curator was in the Test Lab when he looked up to see a man wearing a black rubber apron, boots, and gloves walk by. This man also turned and went into the wall.

The fourth floor is used only by the office staff, who reported hearing phantom music at odd moments. The security personnel would report hearing it late at night, early in the morning, and on weekends, when the fourth floor was not open. It has always been big-band music from the late 1930s and early 1940s. Some of the staff thought it sounded like radio music, but it played only a few seconds and was gone. They wondered if somehow the building were picking up a local radio station, but no radio stations in the Altoona area play big-band music.

A former finance director of the building had a real scare one evening. He punched the button for the elevator to pick him up on the fourth floor late one afternoon. When the doors opened, there was a short old man on the elevator. The man was in dirty bib overalls and had his back to the doors. The finance director stared at the man for a moment, and the old man turned slightly to look back at him. Suddenly the man on the elevator shimmered, faded upward, and was gone.

The finance director ran down the stairs, quite frightened by the apparition. He refused to use the elevator for a few days after his scare. One day he was working on the first floor of the building, when he saw a picture of a group of men working on a steam boiler. In the center of that picture was the man whom he had seen in the elevator.

Through the years, the staff made it a policy to not talk about the ghosts. They accepted that things were going on in the building, but no one would be the first one to say the "G" word. All of that changed one afternoon after a staff meeting. Before the meeting ended, the curator asked if anyone had any other questions or concerns to be addressed. A new employee raised her hand and questioned whether anyone else had ever had any "weird" experiences in the building. She described finding objects moved in the gift shop before opening and piles of toys and books that she had to pick up. As she spoke, the others seemed to break their silence. Suddenly everyone was talking and telling their own ghostly tales.

One of the men who worked security told a story that a secretary verified. One day he received a call from the secretary on the fourth floor, who had a monitor of the various floors of the building at her desk. She had noticed a man on the third floor just standing there for some time. The man seemed to be either confused or lost. After watching the man for a while longer, she radioed to the security man, asking him to go to the third floor and see if the gentleman needed any help. The security man got to the area of the third floor where the man was supposed to be, but he saw nothing. When he radioed up to the secretary for further direction, the woman insisted that he was standing right beside the man.

As the staff changed through the years, the stories persisted. New employees explained their first experiences, and the older personnel quietly confirmed the paranormal antics. No one was truly frightened, but many folks were intrigued by their brushes with the supernatural. Several of the employees were initially skeptics, but few remained that way long.

Perhaps one of the biggest skeptics was the current curator, who simply had never had any paranormal experiences. He took a wait-and-see attitude toward the whole affair, but he was also open-minded enough to allow others to talk about their experiences. Soon he began to have experiences of his own. His first two encounters were with the phantom music on the fourth floor. Being a big-band music fan, he immediately recognized the music type but not the exact song.

Through the years, the new curator has reported hearing the doors open and close and footsteps in the building when he was there alone. Telephones rang from within the building as if someone were calling him from elsewhere in the structure, but he was the only one there.

The visitors on occasion have had paranormal experiences as well. One lady brought her granddaughter to the museum and allowed the child to play in the children's room on the third floor while she used the restroom nearby. When the old woman came out, she clearly heard her little granddaughter talking to someone else and expected to see an adult with her grandchild. Instead, she found the girl totally alone. The little girl insisted she had been talking to a man who had disappeared when her grandmother entered the room. The elderly lady was a bit spooked by this, so they took the elevator down to leave. When the elevator doors opened on the first floor, the little girl ran up to a large, old photograph that caught her eye. She pointed to a tall, lean man and insisted that he was who she had been talking to. The photo was at least fifty years old, and the man was probably in his fifties in that picture. The old woman was so shaken by the experience that she told a staff member her tale.

It seems appropriate that a building dedicated to railroaders is haunted by the men themselves. They play pranks, go about their business, and occasionally are glimpsed by the living. Each floor of the structure has at least one paranormal tale to tell. The museum offers an education in railroading to its visitors, who will come away with a new appreciation of just how hard the work was and how important it was to building this nation. And perhaps they will also walk away with their own ghostly tales to tell.

The Noisy Ghosts of the Red Arrow Wreck

To the earliest explorers and settlers, Pennsylvania must have presented a magnificent, fearsome duality, both alluring and foreboding. As they stood at the edge of Penn's Woods in the early eighteenth century, before them lay a lush, green, bountiful land with clear, rushing streams that had enough strength to spin a waterwheel and produce unlimited power for all the grist- and sawmills a country could need. There was sufficient timber for the construction of hundreds of thousands of homes, both modest and ample, and granite, another building material, lay exposed on the ground. Wild game in abundance supplied families with meat until they cleared enough land to start a farm. But about a third of the way on their journey across Pennsylvania, they would hit a virtual wall of mountains.

There were passes through the northern end of the Blue Ridge Mountains, accessible by horse and mule-powered wagons, but when the railroads began to make their way across the state, some of the mountains proved too formidable. An early-nineteenth-century trip from Philadelphia to Pittsburgh would often include a mule-drawn canal boat, stagecoach, horseback, and the railroad, which consumed as much as three and a half days. Railroad engineers began to bore tunnels through the mountains, a time-consuming, dangerous enterprise.

The area near Altoona presented them with an interesting challenge, which they solved by building a giant, horseshoe-shaped curve in the tracks. Irish immigrants completed the curve in 1854. It's a 220-degree looping curve, 1,800 feet across and 2,375 feet in length. From one end to the other, it rises 122 feet. During World War II, it was third on Adolf Hitler's list of things in America he wanted sabotaged and therefore was guarded by the military around the clock. At one point, saboteurs were on their way to dynamite it when they were captured. Today it is used by up to fifty trains a day and is billed as the "Eighth Wonder of the Modern World."

Not far from Horseshoe Curve is a lesser-known area called Bennington Curve, just outside of Gallitzen. This curve is not as tight as the famous Horseshoe Curve, a few miles down the track, but it is flanked by a steep drop-off.

In 1947, World War II had been over for less than two years. The nation as a whole was getting back to normal. The country was back at work. The Depression-era kids had grown up. Tempered by a second world war, they were home and feeling safe. There was still a certain romanticism about the railroads. Before airline travel became so popular, they were the prime method of getting around the country. Soldiers had traveled tens of thousands of miles across the country to military training schools and back again. Many had ridden trains on their postwar honeymoons.

In a romantic tradition, the railroads gave their trains names. The one that approached Bennington Curve on the frigid day of February 18, 1947, was called the Red Arrow. This passenger express train headed out of the Gallitzen Tunnels, just a couple miles from the great Horseshoe Curve. Had it been a little closer to the curve, it would have had to slow to safely round the tight bend.

Instead, as it rounded the Bennington Curve, it suddenly jumped the track and careened wildly down into a gully, the cars twisting like a dismembered snake. Twenty-four passengers were killed and 131 injured in one of the worst train wrecks ever on the Pennsylvania Railroad. Black-and-white photos taken at the time of the wreck show the frozen horror: Two men dwarfed beneath a car lying sideways across another car, the letters "ennsyl" visible but ominously upside down; the local coroner in his long dress coat and fashionable fedora hat, lifting a blanket on an old-fashioned stretcher and peering under it to confirm the death of a man whose shoes emerge from the other end of the blanket; rescuers lowering a minister from a car hanging sideways over the rim of the curve, his duties to the dead in the car completed.

It is said that if you park near one of the tunnels in the dark of the night and flash your headlights three times, then extinguish them, you will hear what is clearly impossible: invisible people laughing and muttering. If you can gather the courage to look outside your car windows, there, emerging from the darkness and moving slowly toward you, will be the shadows of the people who died in the twisted wreck of the Red Arrow.

Haunted Mishler Theater

Built by Isaac Mishler in 1906 in the city of Altoona, the Mishler Theater has seen quite a bit of life. The grand theater opened on February 15, 1906, and burned down on October 19 of that same year. Isaac Mishler was devastated. He had worked in the theater his whole life, and the Mishler Theater was his dream. After gathering the money together to rebuild his dream, he was so dedicated to reopening the theater that he had crews work round the clock for a month to restore the building to its former grandeur. The workmen succeeded admirably. The result of Isaac's vision and the workers' talent can still be seen today. From the plush red seats to the gilted ornate murals painted on the ceiling of the building, the theater is a work of art in the Baroque style.

Over the years, the building's fortunes ebbed and flowed. In the theater's heyday, people such as Al Jolson entertained there. When live plays were no longer in vogue, the Mishler became a movie house.

During its darker days, the theater was left to fall apart. It was slated for the wrecking ball until the Blair County Arts Foundation entered the picture. Through the work of several people, the old building was saved.

Today a trip to the Mishler Theater is like stepping back in time. The building once more sports the plush red seats, secluded ornate boxes for the wealthy, and breathtaking murals on the ceiling. Once more the ghost light, a light kept burning on the stage when it's not being used, is illuminated. Live actors again tread the boards, carrying on a tradition that an old theater like the Mishler can be proud of, and it would appear that ghosts are walking the boards too.

It was during the restoration that people began having supernatural experiences. As often happens with hauntings, people did not mention these things at first. But soon plays were being produced, and the casts and crews of the shows began to have their own encounters. The paranormal events at the Mishler Theater began to be talked about.

The most commonly reported spirit sighted there is that of old Isaac Mishler. His office was once on the second level off stage right. He would come out onto the first balcony and stand there to watch rehearsals and performances. Late at night, crews working onstage in the theater have noticed a man watching them from above. Several people have recognized this man as Isaac Mishler from the portrait of him that hangs in the ticket area.

But Isaac apparently is not happy merely watching the goings-on from above. He or someone else has been known to sit several rows back in the center of the theater to watch as directors hold rehearsals. More than one person has seen the seat in that area depress and stay down seemingly by itself, even though the seats are spring-loaded and stay up until the weight of a person holds them down.

One director was sitting in this area as he directed a rehearsal and felt a hand on his shoulder from behind. He turned, fully expecting a friend to be there, but was shocked to find no one.

Late one evening, some of the staffers were working and realized that the caretaker was waiting for them before he could go. As the woman and her friend worked out front, they saw booted feet walk by the back of the stage, and the curtain rippled as if someone were moving behind it. The woman assumed that it was the caretaker, because he was the only other person in the theater. She called out to him, "We'll be done and get out of here in a minute."

The figure behind the curtain never paused, but to her shock, the caretaker yelled from the back of the auditorium: "That's okay, take your time. I'm in no hurry." The woman whirled around to see the caretaker's head sticking out of the ticket booth area.

This woman has spent a good bit of time at the theater, and her daughter has grown up there. As a small child, the girl would often talk about the old man she saw. One day, when another employee who has had psychic experiences all her life was there, she began talking to the little girl about the old man. She and the child's mother took her into the ticket booth, where the child immediately fastened on the picture of Isaac Mishler. "That's him," she told them. "That's the old man that I saw." The psychic had suspected as much. She had often seen Isaac in the building, and she suspected that the child was seeing him too.

Many other employees also have stories to tell of looking up to see Isaac watching them or hearing footsteps above them on the catwalks when no one was up there. One of the men who run the curtains and sets in the theater claims that one night he watched as some of the ropes untied themselves and lowered slowly to adjust a set.

It is speculated that Isaac Mishler is not the only spirit still in the theater. Years ago, an elderly gentleman helped manage the place, and the Mishler Theater was the center of his world. He'd come in early each day, go out for lunch, and return to the theater until suppertime. He was there five days a week. As the gentleman grew older, he became very hard of hearing. One day he went to cross the busy street outside of the theater and did not hear a car as it bore down on him. The car struck the old man, and he was badly injured.

As the employee recovered from his injuries, his family decided he should no longer be allowed to make his own decisions. He was too old and frail, and he certainly could not return to work at the Mishler Theater. The gentleman was taken from the hospital to a nursing home to finish recovering. He longed to return to his former life, but it was made very clear that he would never get to go back. As time went by, he became ever more depressed by the situation, until he finally passed away. After his death, the old gentleman was cremated, as was his wish.

A few weeks after his funeral, one of his nieces who shared his passion for the Mishler Theater came in with a large bag. She spent the day working there and kept about her business. According to the staff, when she left that day, her bag was empty. Folks have always wondered whether she might have brought her uncle's ashes to the theater where he had loved to be. It would have been his wish to spend eternity at the Mishler, and some people believe he just might be doing so.

One of the most haunted areas in the theater is the second-floor balcony. It is used as the lighting area, and during shows or dress rehearsals, one of the ghosts in the theater seems to enjoy playing tricks on the lighting staff. There have been many reports of people feeling touched, hearing footsteps, and glimpsing a presence beside them as they work the light board.

The reports of incidents in the lighting area of the second-floor balcony increase when young people work there. It seems that Isaac enjoys teasing young folks, who have reported some of the strongest phenomena up there. Some have said that someone touched them on the neck and brushed or patted their hair.

One night a few years ago, two young men and a young woman were working the lighting board for a show. The young woman seemed to be particularly susceptible to being touched and insisted that someone was stroking her hair and caressing her neck. The two young men reported that they felt someone brush their backs, but no one was behind them. The girl was very scared; in fact, she was so upset about it that she threatened to quit.

A longtime staff member was changing out lights far above the theater stage one day. She was in a device called a cherry picker, which raises a person up to the ceiling. The device is on wheels and can be rolled from one lighting fixture to another by someone on the ground. The woman's husband was pushing the cherry picker along for her. When she finished a light about halfway down the row, she felt him push her on to the next light. She called out, "Thank you," and looked down. No one was near the cherry picker. Her husband heard her voice and called out from backstage that he'd move her in a moment. He had wandered off to take care of a small task while he waited to move her to the next fixture. When the woman got down, she told her husband about the ghostly helper who had rolled the cart along for her.

The Mishler Theater is a living piece of history. So many people, first Isaac and then others, put a lot of time and passion into the theater. It was more than just a building to them, and maybe they are there behind the scenes, still making sure the theater is running smoothly for all to enjoy.

Strange Goings-On at Baker Mansion

The stone Greek Revival mansion that sits in Mansion Park near the ball field in Altoona recalls a bygone era. The large, semicircular driveway swings gracefully around the back of the mansion, where the builder, Elias Baker, used to receive business associates. The mansion was built in 1849 and was the grandest structure in the area at the time. Some of the local folks called the mansion "Baker's Folly," because they thought Elias had spent beyond his means to build the edifice, but the businessman seemed not to care that he was always in debt. He had a taste for the finer things in life and a taste for land, which he purchased as often as he could.

Elias Baker had made a fortune running the Allegheny Furnace, which produced iron. Elias and his cousin, Mr. Diller, had purchased the furnace and 3,373 acres of land in 1836. For several years, Elias lived near the furnace that he and he cousin ran. He eventually bought out his cousin's interest in the furnace and decided to build a fine mansion for his family. Elias was dealing in the iron industry when it was at its apex. With the building of the Pennsylvania Canal system and the Portage Railroad, his product could be transported to the more lucrative markets in Lancaster, Carlisle, and Philadelphia.

Elias Baker was not a man who scrimped on his personal luxuries, and his home was appointed with the finest materials. The large double parlor was furnished with a hand-carved suite from Belgium. The entire house was appointed with marble mantels shipped from Italy, and plenty of iron was used in the construction of the building.

Elias and his wife, Hetty Woods Baker, raised three children, Sylvester, Anna, and David. By some accounts, Elias was a good husband and father, but others claimed that he was a difficult man who expected his own way about everything. Certainly some of the stories that became part of the lore of Baker Mansion indicate that at the very least, Elias Baker was unyielding and socially discriminating.

David was the only one of Elias's children to ever marry. He died in an accident and left behind a wife and one little daughter. Sylvester never married, but there were rumors that he had an affair with a maid in the house with whom he fell in love. As the story goes, when the young woman was with child, Sylvester told his father of his indiscretions. Supposedly, Elias sent the young woman away but sent money for years to support the child she had.

Another, similar story has long been associated with Elias's daughter, Anna. She was said to have fallen in love with one of the men who worked the iron furnace. She and the young man were desperately in love, and the young man asked her to marry him. He gave her an engagement ring as proof of his love. When Anna spoke to her father about the matter, he told her that the young man was a gold digger and the ring was probably not real. To prove to her father that the diamond was real, Anna carved her initials in the glass of one of the windows in the double parlor. That glass remained in the building until recent years.

Elias was socially conscious and would not tolerate his daughter marrying a common laborer. He threatened Anna, but she held fast to her plans. Eventually he had the young man Anna loved brought before him. He explained to the young fellow that Anna was not prepared to marry a common laborer. She did not know how to care for a house, cook, clean, and live like a poor woman. If the young man married Anna, Elias assured him, she would never be allowed to see her family again. She would be banished from her world of wealth and influence, and she would not be accepted in his world either.

Elias painted a terrible picture of what life for Anna and the young man would be like. Then he asked the young man how much money it would take to make him go away. It is said that the young man took a check and left, and Anna never saw her young lover again.

Anna's heart was broken. She vowed to her father and herself that if she could not marry the man she loved, she would not marry at all. Anna kept that vow and died in 1914 in her home, still a spinster. She would be the last Baker to live in the house.

The Baker family heirs rented the house to the Blair County Historical Society in 1922, and the building was first opened as a museum at that time. By 1941, the society had purchased the house and grounds. Today the house is home to many historical artifacts from the region. In the dining room is one of the few remaining relics of the War Governors Conference, held at the Logan Hotel in Altoona: the large, round table where the governors of each Union state gave a vow to support Lincoln to the conclusion of the Civil War.

The Double Parlor and Single Parlor across the hall house Baker family treasures and are much the way they had been in the days of Elias and Anna. Elias's office still exists and is used as an entry area for visitors. The second and third floors house a variety of objects from around the area. Antiques stand side by side with guns from various wars, and on the third floor are storage and research materials.

One of the most famous objects in the house, from a paranormal perspective, is a wedding dress kept in a locked glass case in Anna's small winter bedroom. A contemporary of Anna's named Elizabeth Bell wore the beautiful Victorian wedding gown, which was donated by the Bell family. According to local lore, Anna and Elizabeth did not get along in life, and Anna resents having Elizabeth's dress in her bedroom. What bigger insult could there be for a young woman who never got to be with her loved one than to see a rival's wedding gown every day for eternity and remember that she had been denied her own wedding?

It is said that the wedding dress moves inside the case as if being fanned out by someone and that the parasol and slippers change position. Some people believe that Anna is touching the objects, but a few folks believe that the spirit who moves the dress is Elizabeth. According to a former curator, Elizabeth Bell did not like Anna and enjoyed taunting her about being a spinster throughout her life.

Anna, however, does not haunt just the little winter bedroom. Her spirit has been seen throughout the house as well. Several summers ago, two tour guides were working in the building before it opened for the day. Both were dressed in period costume. The female guide was working on some materials on the third floor, while the male guide was working on an exhibit on the second floor. As the male guide stepped into the hallway, he saw a woman in black round the stairs downward to the first floor. He leaned over the banister to call to his female associate. The woman did not respond to him, so the man called out again as she disappeared around a corner on the first floor. Above him, his female associate leaned over the banister to inquire what her partner wanted. The man was quite surprised. A search of the building yielded no strangers. The male guide believes to this day that he saw Anna Baker hurrying down the stairs.

According to newspaper accounts, a local radio station, WRTA, once did a Halloween broadcast from the mansion and brought along a paranormal expert from St. Louis named Gordon Hainer. Hainer excused himself to visit the restroom during a break. He went upstairs, and then suddenly he was heard pounding back down the steps, hitting about every fourth step on the way. A very upset Hainer burst into the room where the broadcast equipment was set up. He said he had felt a presence on the second step of the staircase up to the third floor. According to Hainer, the presence was watching him and knew he did not belong in the building. The presence wanted him to leave, and the feeling frightened him.

In the early 1980s, *Life* magazine featured Baker Mansion in an article, "The Ten Most Haunted Houses in the Nation." During their visit, the magazine staff reported more problems with their equipment here than they had at any other site. Their strobes would not work, and eventually they had to cobble together one strobe from two. They had problems with photographing the wedding dress and had to use a good bit of film to get that one shot.

Anna Baker has been reported to haunt every room in the house, but none more consistently than the master bedroom, which she took over after her parents' death. She has been seen in the room on occasion, and a photograph of mist rising from the floor and forming just in front of a dress of Anna's was captured several years ago.

The haunting of Baker Manson manifests in several ways. Ever since 1942, a disturbing odor has come and gone from the house. It is a terrible smell, and no source has ever been found for it. Years may pass between occurrences, but the smell always appears in the same place in the house, and no one can mistake the odor for anything else.

Some say a small marble table on the second floor has become too hot to touch on occasion. According to a former curator, a Regina music box has played despite not being wound. A lap harp was once reportedly thrown more than twenty feet across a room when no one was even standing close to it. There have been other stories of doors locking and unlocking, shadowy shapes flitting through the halls, and a feeling of being watched and not wanted.

Once two women were cleaning the delicate crystal chandelier in the dining room, with one woman up the ladder and the other steadying it. The woman holding the ladder suddenly noticed that the room was very cold, and then she felt something hit her hard. She shouted and jumped back. The woman on the ladder hurried down.

Cold spots have often been reported in the building. During an evening of ghostly entertainment one Halloween recently, a guest reported feeling very cold in the dining room. A device was brought in to measure the temperature, and the room was 54 degrees, though the rest of the house was at a comfortable 74 degrees. A few moments later, the cold dissipated and the room returned to the normal temperature.

During that same evening, there were several other interesting phenomena. Two people on the second floor heard a scratching sound from inside a wooden cabinet in Sylvester's old bedroom. They turned to look, as the door swung slowly open. Despite their best efforts, the two could not find any reasonable explanation.

In a narrow hallway on the third floor, a young woman insisted that something was pulling her hair. Three of her companions turned back to look at her, and her ponytail was standing straight up in the air as if grabbed and pulled up by some unseen force.

In the basement, a banging was heard in the storage cellar through which water flows to keep perishables cool. There is virtually nothing in the storage cellar, and no explanation could be found for the loud, clear bangs.

The staff members have the most interesting stories to tell. They believe that along with Anna, her brother Sylvester also haunts the house. Sylvester did not ever marry either, but he did run the family business until just before his death.

At one time, the security system at Baker Manson included pressure pads under the carpeting. When the system was turned on and someone stepped on a pressure pad, the alarm would go off at the local police station. On several occasions, the pressure pad security system went off. Each time this happened, the curator was called in to unlock the building while the police checked out the structure. No one was ever found in the building during these night-time checks. However, once a police officer brought in his trained police dog to help in the search. The dog obediently checked the office, dining room, and double parlor without incident, but at the doorway to the single parlor on the other side of the main hall, he froze. Despite commands from his handler, the dog would not enter the room. He stopped and growled into what was an empty room but would not budge. The dog finally had to be taken out.

Interestingly enough, that same single parlor is said by the staff to be the center of Sylvester's activities. On the last night of his life, Sylvester was lying on the sofa in the room while he was being read to. He stood up to go upstairs to his room and collapsed with a heart attack. He died on the floor just in front of the sofa, which is still in the room today.

One other incident happened with the pressure pads in that room. At one point, the one in front of the sofa had to be replaced because a sensor had been crushed. Something heavy had fallen on it during the late-evening hours while no one was in the building. No object was found on the sensor. To make things even more mysterious, no one can walk on the carpet in the room; the display is roped off in order to preserve the precious carpeting.

The former staffers have many tales to tell. One tour guide told a story of his own encounter with Sylvester. During the last part of Sylvester's life, he walked with a cane and often would pound on the floor to get the attention of the staff if he wanted something. Sylvester often took lunch in his room and did not go downstairs until later in the day. One day, the rest of the staff had gone out for dinner, but this guide had chosen to stay behind and study. Just after a clock struck the noon hour, he heard a loud tap-tap from above. Mentally he located the sound, and it was in Sylvester's old room. The tour guide's first thought was that someone either had stayed behind or was playing a joke on him. The young man shut his book and went upstairs, but he saw nothing. He paused in the bedroom where Sylvester's cane was kept. Something about the room was out of sorts.

Suddenly it hit him: The cane was on the bed and not behind the door where it belonged. The guide had run the last tour before lunch and certainly would have noticed the out-of-place cane if it had been on the bed at that time. He always paused in the room for some time to talk about Sylvester. The tour guide believes that an impatient Sylvester was tapping for his lunch, which was to be served sharply at noon.

One guide claims that in 1995, she and two other guides were working in the children's room, filled with toys from the past, when they saw a big ball of white light zip through the room. The light seemed to attach itself to the wall and stayed there. The guides tried to find a rational explanation, such as car lights or reflections, but they could not locate a source for the light. Several minutes later, as suddenly as it had come, the light vanished.

Another guide insists that when he was in the Lincoln Room, a room dedicated to memorabilia from President Lincoln, footsteps came up behind him. The young man knew he was alone in the locked building, and he feared turning around to see who was so close to him. Instead, he sidestepped and hurried around the room and out without turning back to see who or what was in the room with him.

At one time, the staff kept a journal of the unusual phenomena. Entries from the book include incidents of furniture moving, disembodied footsteps, and pounding noises. A man's voice was heard by a tour guide who had worked there for many years and was not afraid of any entities in the building. The guides logged temperature drops, the dress moving, and a rocker in the master bedroom moving on its own. Guides also wrote of being touched, pushed, and seeing apparitions. A male with short, dark hair parted in the middle was seen in the master bedroom. Other guides wrote of feeling depressed and lonely in the master bedroom. The feelings were not their own, and they could sense that they were experiencing someone else's emotions.

The strangest tales come not from the staff, however, but the guests who have toured the building. These people often profess not to know the stories of the house, and their experiences have been startling.

In 1976, during the gas shortage, high prices and long lines made travel difficult, so the curator at Baker Mansion decided that summer would be a good time to finish much-needed renovations to the building. The decision was made not to open for the summer.

One day a woman came to the building. She was disappointed to learn that she could not tour the mansion. She explained to the staff that she had been hoping for several years to see the house when she was in town. In fact, she had stayed a day longer in hopes of finally visiting the mansion. The staff explained the situation but told her they would show her through the parts of the building not under renovation if she would like. They truly hated to send her away unhappy after she made a special trip just to see the house.

As the tour began, the woman was excited and happy. But going up the stairs, she suddenly got very upset and insisted on going back down. On the first floor again, the woman calmed down and told the tour guide that she had seen someone upstairs watching her, and the person did not want her there. The woman apologized but refused to go back on the tour.

One of most interesting and disturbing stories was from several years ago, when a woman from out of town had car problems just outside the mansion late one evening. She walked up to the house because she saw lights inside and knocked on the door. Something knocked back at her, but no one came to the door. The woman was angry and upset by the experience, believing that someone in that house was quite rude.

The next day, the woman returned to the house and asked to speak to the curator. She explained the incident and demanded to know who had been on duty the night before that was so rude. The curator explained that the mansion was locked up at night and no one was inside—except for the ghosts of Anna and Sylvester. The woman was more upset when she left than when she had arrived at Baker Mansion that day. She had unwittingly stumbled into the history of the many haunted experiences of Baker Mansion.

Sideling Hill's Spooky CCC Camp

In 1929, the United States stock market crashed. Millions upon millions of dollars were suddenly lost. Men who woke up wealthy suddenly found themselves destitute. Financiers and bankers committed suicide. If the wealthy were no longer wealthy, then the poor were almost beyond help. This began a dark period for the United States known today as the Great Depression.

The nation ached, and anger built up at the government for what the people were living through. Men lost their jobs, families lost their homes, people were starving, and there was a great sense of desperation and frustration. It was obvious that the nation was not going to easily pull out of the Depression. It would take many years for the nation to heal naturally.

During the election of 1933, the Depression was the major political issue. Republican president Herbert Hoover took the brunt of the blame. His Democratic challenger, Franklin D. Roosevelt, offered up what he called the 100-Day Plan. After his election, Roosevelt was as good as his word, and he rolled up his sleeves and began setting up programs designed to give relief to the people of this nation and restore hope, faith, and dignity.

Roosevelt realized that many of the poor were not people who wanted a handout; they wanted a hand up. These people wanted to work for pay, not just receive stopgap help from the government. For the adults, he created the Works Progress Administration (WPA). For families without an able-bodied adult male who could participate, Roosevelt designed another program, the Civilian Conservation Corps (CCC), for males aged thirteen to nineteen. They would go to work camps, where they would improve public forest lands, do road work, and help build dams and other public works. The boys would be given training, food, shelter, and clothes. They would receive $8 per month for working eight hours a day, five days a week, and an additional $20 per month would be sent back home to help their families. Young men and boys lined up to sign up for the CCC. The money was desperately needed, and so was the work.

In Pennsylvania, CCC camps were set up all over the state, and through the hard work of those young men and boys, we now have some beautiful state parks.

In Buchanan State Forest, CCC Camp No. S-52 was set up at Sideling Hill in 1933. While it was in operation, hundreds of young men and boys lived at the camp. They broke the roads and trails that people still use today. After the camp was shut down, it was nearly forgotten until 1940, when it was pressed back into service by the U.S. Army. World War II was in full swing, and the Army refurbished the camp to house conscientious objectors and draftees who would not fight in the war.

The camp saw service for a few years, but then the government decided to move the conscientious objectors and place German prisoners of war in the camp. Barbed-wire fencing was strung and buildings were modified for this more sinister use. German prisoners were brought in and housed at the remote, wooded site. During that time, two German prisoners supposedly were killed when they were moving rocks to build a stone wall and the rock pile fell on the men. It was a tragic accident, and it kept those men from returning to their homeland and their families.

After World War II was over, the camp was disbanded, and slowly the forest began to reclaim it. Trees took over, and the buildings moldered and rotted. They were torn apart, knocked down, or just gave way over time. All that remains as testimony to the past are a few foundations, a single great chimney from the cook's hall, and a few scattered piles of stone that obviously marked a building entrance long ago. The pipes that crisscrossed the shower room stick up through the grass and dead leaves. The shower house has been reduced to a single small wall that one can easily step over.

Today there are stories that some of the old CCC camp's former inhabitants never left those woods. Sideling Hill is not a tourist attraction, and people do not drive long distances to visit, because there is nothing to do there but enjoy the woods. Many locals, however, drive the gravel road to spend time in the woods that circle them. Some park their cars to wander among the ruins of the buildings and soak up the charm of this forgotten place. Occasionally some of these folks have reported seeing two men in strange uniforms in the distance stacking rocks. When the men are approached, they simply disappear. Others have reported a man in an old, ragged prisoner's uniform running up to them. The man spoke in German, then faded away before their astonished eyes.

Other stories date farther back, to the days when it was a CCC camp. Some people say they have come across young men digging and cutting trees, who simply fade away when approached. Who are the men? No one knows their names, but those who have witnessed them insist that they are the spirits of some of those young men who worked at the CCC camp so long ago.

At dusk, the shadows lengthen, the deer begin to move, the chipmunks and squirrels cease their chattering, and the turkeys call a nightly greeting from the trees as they settle in. As the shadows lengthen and shift, the ghosts of long ago seem to come out to work and laugh and relive old times at this little abandoned camp.

Northern Pennsylvania

The portion of Pennsylvania that most retains the rugged flavor of the territory the earliest settlers knew is the northern part of the state. Spring brings fresh, spirited streams to life. The chill in the forests holds on until early summer. And when summer comes, it is with a rush of vitality, embracing everything with the sultry breath of nature.

Vast slabs of mountains covered in harlequin colors in the fall follow the traces of streams that, by the time they reach the southeastern part of Pennsylvania, will become the broad Susquehanna. By late fall, deer in abundance draw hunters from several states to the area to winnow the herds, now blending ghostlike, virtually invisible, among the grays and browns of the unmeasured woods.

And it is from these dark regions that dark stories emerge. In northern Pennsylvania, the sparse population means that if you are unfortunate enough to encounter one of the bizarre and often unfriendly supernatural entities residing there, you are likely to do it alone.

The Ax Hollow Murders

Ghost stories, folklore, and legends often blend seamlessly, making it impossible to tell where one ends and the other begins. In the area outside Erie, an old legend was born from an all too tragic event. It is the story of the Ax Hollow murders and the haunting this tragedy spawned. Over the years, this story has changed, as young men saw it as a way to frighten their girlfriends. But going back in time, one can trace out the bare framework of the original tale.

At one time, there was a small working farm on the road known as Ax Hollow. The farmer who worked the ground there was a dour man who never seemed to find any joy in life. His was a dark world, where no one laughed or had joy. It was hard for those who loved him. His wife had become a shadow of a person. There was no romance or love in her life. Hers was a world of work and keeping her husband from being angry. The children, too, suffered because of their father's dark way of looking at the world. They went to school, came home and worked, and were allowed little time to enjoy the boundless world around them.

Everything changed one summer when the man hired a drifter as help for the summer farming season. The fellow slept in the barn but always had a smile on his lips and song in his heart. He was quiet but went around humming to himself because he knew his singing annoyed the farmer. It was as if anything with a spark of joy and light had to be extinguished before the dour man. But for the hired man, joy just seemed to come naturally, and he secretly brightened up the world for the little family. He'd send the children in with a beautiful flower that he found while working a field. He'd make a little toy to please the children and hurry to do a few of their chores before they got home so that they had time to play. All of this was done behind the farmer's back. The man would fret and scream and punish the family if they let him know they found joy in something the hired hand did.

The farmer probably would have fired the hired man if he could have, but the fellow worked cheaply and did good work. He simply could not justify firing the man.

Perhaps the poor housewife was charmed into infidelity, or perhaps nothing more than kindness transpired between the hired hand and the woman, but the farmer began to suspect that his wife was having an affair with the man. The farmer watched and brooded, until he finally drove the hired hand off. That same day, he confronted his wife. His anger was immense, and in his fury, he picked up an ax and swung it at her. He hacked her to death, but still his rage was not abated. He turned the ax on his children and destroyed them too.

The story states that he was found in the hollow where the road dips down between two large hills, still carrying the ax and muttering to himself. Some people thought he was looking for the hired man; others believed that he was trying to flee the grisly scene in his home. Perhaps he didn't even know where he was or what he had done. In any case, he surrendered easily enough, and he saved the county the trouble of a trial by committing suicide on his first night in the jail.

That seems to be the original story that circulated long ago. Since then, the story has mutated into an urban legend. It is said that if a young couple parks along the lonely road, the farmer will appear outside the windows of the car swinging his bloody ax. Other versions say that the farmer makes a noise so that the young man in the car will get out, and then he kills them both.

It is easy to dismiss such tales, but then there are other stories that come every so often, such as when a startled motorist insists that he saw a man covered in blood and carrying an ax walking along the road as if in a daze. These people are not thrill seekers, but rather just people going about their business until they stumble into the middle of an impossible urban legend and see it come to life.

Specters at John Brown's Tannery

John Brown was an ordinary man who never imagined that he would become one of the most controversial figures in American history. He never dreamed that fate would propel him into the national spotlight, nor did he ever think that he'd be both hated and revered by an entire nation. John Brown was just a regular man who wanted to make a life for his wife and children. He was a prosperous businessman, a respected member of his community, and a pillar of his church. He was the most respectable of men when he lived in Crawford County, Pennsylvania, and ran his tannery.

John Brown came to Meadville area of Pennsylvania with his wife of five years, Dianthe Lusk. The couple and their three small boys settled in the village of New Richmond, where they started a tannery. The tannery employed fifteen men, and Brown, a big, strapping fellow who was known for his honest ways and hard work, harvested and sold lumber and ran his farm. He was prospering in the community.

At twenty-six years old, Brown had already become an ardent abolitionist. He was a man who lived his beliefs, and he had a secret room built in the tannery to house runaway slaves. Brown's tannery became a regular stop on the Underground Railroad. He knew he was risking a lot for strangers, but his faith would allow him to do no less.

Brown's first wife died giving birth to their seventh child. He soon wed a sixteen-year-old named Mary Day, with whom he had thirteen children. Brown began the first local post office and became its first postmaster. He also started the Independent Congressional Society, because he felt that the six-mile drive to the local church was too much.

Eventually the tannery began to sink into debt, and Brown realized that he was losing his business. In 1835, he took his family to Ohio to start over, leaving behind the tannery and his dream business. He also left behind the best time of his life. The tannery building became a cheese factory, a gristmill, and a jelly factory before it burned down in 1907. The ruins of the building are preserved today as a testament to John Brown's life.

Stories of hauntings have long circled elusively around the tannery site. People claim to have seen a tall, strapping man moving among the ruins. Others say that they hear voices while they are there alone. Yet other folks claim to see and hear a black man there, who seems to shift silently at dawn and dusk. Could he have been a slave who died en route to freedom? It is also said that bodies are buried near the tannery, and some believe the tannery's ghosts are held there by the passion that shaped John Brown's life. Could one of the ghosts be the spirit of John Brown? Has he returned to the place and time when he was a prosperous businessman, family man, and churchman? Does he long for that simple life before his sons were killed and he felt forced to defend his beliefs? Whispered words, ghostly footsteps, and walking shadows have all been reported at the tannery, and if it is the spirit of John Brown, he seems unaware that he was destined to help change his nation.

Edgar Allen Poe and the Eutaw House

No discussion of Pennsylvania's paranormal would be complete without the story of Edgar Allan Poe, the dark, mysterious, doomed genius of nineteenth-century American literature. Poe was the master of the macabre, and it was no doubt a result of his tragic childhood.

Born in 1809, he was only three years old when both parents died. His godfather, an affluent Richmond businessman named John Allan, took Edgar into his home, then to England and Scotland for his early education. He was brought back to Richmond in 1820 and entered the University of Virginia in 1826. But there were demons in his life even then, and a dispute with his godfather over Edgar's gambling habit caused him to leave the university after only eight months. He enlisted in the Army, was discharged upon the death of his foster mother, but gained an appointment to the United States Military Academy at West Point in 1830. But West Point is not a place for one with even slight disciplinary problems, and Poe was expelled for numerous minor infractions. In the meantime, his first poems were published.

Poe moved to Baltimore to live with his aunt Maria Clemm and ended up marrying his thirteen-year-old cousin, Virginia Clemm. But he was haunted by personal demons, and he lost his job as an editor because of hard drinking. He lived in Philadelphia from 1838 to 1844, then moved to New York, where he edited magazines and wrote stories and poetry. Finally, in 1845, with the publication of *The Raven and Other Poems,* his fame was solidified. But tragedy stalked him, and Virginia died just two years later. In 1849 in Richmond, he became engaged to a childhood sweetheart. Traveling north to bring Mrs. Clemm to the wedding, he spent a drunken evening in Baltimore, which cost him his life. The demons had finally won.

In Center County east of State College is Poe Valley, evidently named after some cousins of the famous Poe, for he was on his way there in 1839 to administer to a cousin's estate after the relative's death in Poe Valley. Poe's luggage, so the story goes, had been lost along the way, and he stayed the night in Potter's Mills at the Eutaw House, a stage stop with a long history.

James Potter had served in the French and Indian War and on General George Washington's staff during the Revolution. Potter built a log house to serve as a stage stop, then constructed some mills. He called the stage stop the Eutaw House after the local Indians. The town became known to travelers as Potter's Mills, the name it bears today.

After his death in 1789, Potter's family apparently demolished the old log cabin and built a new one near its foundation. For well over a hundred years, it provided rest and succor to travelers through the mountains of Pennsylvania. In 1939, it was purchased by Centre County native Harrison Edgar Shawley, who stumbled upon the old "Eutaw House" sign in the attic and subsequently resurrected the old name and restored the old building.

It is from Shawley's memory that the Poe connection emanates. Shawley insisted that during Poe's stay in 1839, the writer met and fell in love with a beautiful local mountain girl. That Shawley recalled the name of the young woman, Helena Hallferty Park, lends credence to the tale. Poe wrote at least two poems "To Helen," but it is doubtful that they refer to Helena. The character Lenore in *The Raven*, however, is, according to Shawley, based on the lovely mountain girl.

In the course of Poe's short stay at Eutaw House, the story goes, Helena broke his sensitive heart. On a lonely walk up the mountain to Raven's Knob, Poe watched as the black birds dove and circled. Their plaintive *caw-caw* touched his own anguished soul, thus planting the seeds for his most famous poem. According to legend, he even left his initials carved on one of the tables in the Eutaw House, though anyone could have scratched the "E. A. P." into the ancient wood over the century and a half.

Numerous bizarre stories surround the Eutaw House and seem to stem from a few legends that date back to its very beginning as a stagecoach stop. With no method to call ahead, there was no telling who or what might show up at the doorstep of a stagecoach stop. Thus one night, a prison wagon pulled in to the stop, and the prisoner was locked in a room in the attic for the night. Two versions exist of his story. One says that he tried to escape and was shot and brought back to the attic to die. The other maintains that he was despondent at his hopeless fate and hanged himself from a rafter rather than continue his incarceration. Local paranormal investigators have photographed light orbs, which they believe to be the unsettled remnants of a human soul, in the attic area of the Eutaw House.

Another story has it that local Indian tribes periodically raided the Eutaw House stables for horses kept there overnight by the travelers. Finally one of the raiders was captured. As an example to the raiding Indians, he was hanged from a large tree at the corner of the property. Researchers have spoken to members of the Shawleys' staff at the Eutaw House. After hours, they would congregate for drinks on the second-floor balcony off the ballroom. On particularly windy nights, they would hear a strange, unique creaking coming from the huge, old tree on the corner of the property. It sounded, they swore, like a rope, burdened with a heavy load, groaning around one of the branches. Added to this already strange auditory experience was the sound of an ominous soft thudding against the trunk of the tree. Some courageous employees investigated, but no source of the noise could be found. They confirmed that it sounded exactly the way a human body would sound as it bumped up against the tree.

Others have reported supernatural phenomena inside. As with all restaurants, the tables were cleaned and set at night for the next day's customers. Yet nearly every morning, employees found one of the tables rearranged as if three diners had used it for a late-night meal.

Perhaps that relates to the sightings of a little girl in various places both inside the building and outside in the yard. Mostly, however, she is seen on the main stairs. Witnesses agree that she appears to be about seven years old. Occasionally she is accompanied by an older woman clothed in what appears to be a black mourning dress, who has been named by the staff the Woman in Black. Some have reported hearing the sounds of footsteps along the hallways where no one can be seen walking. As if they need to be able to see where they are going, the specters turn lights on and off. Lights also come on in the room that Poe allegedly used during his stay here—long after hours and when no one is in the room. Could it be that Poe's otherworldly inspiration for ghastly tales still abides beyond his mortal existence?

But perhaps the most disturbing phenomena is when staff and guests occasionally have their quiet conversations interrupted by the sound of a little girl crying softly. One can only speculate what could have happened in life that caused a woman to mourn and a little girl to sob pitifully long after death.

Perhaps it is the Woman in Black and the little girl who are using the table after the doors are locked, but who could the third after-hours diner be? Some of the staff at the Eutaw House think they know. They have occasionally seen the misty shadow of a man walking with the little girl and the Woman in Black, both inside and outside the house. He has been described as a slim, almost delicate-looking man with dark features and a thin, dark moustache. A man who resembles the ancient daguerreotype of one of America's greatest authors, Edgar Allan Poe.

Clinton County's Headless Frenchman

Etienne Brulé was a French adventurer who first arrived in North America at age sixteen as a scout for Samuel de Champlain around 1608. In 1610, he was sent by Champlain to live with the Algonquin Indians to learn their language and ways. In 1611, he was sent to do the same thing with the Huron Indians living near Lake Huron. In 1615, on another mission from Champlain, he became the first European to reach Lake Ontario, and in the same year, he traced the Susquehanna River from its headwaters to the Chesapeake Bay.

America in the early 1600s still belonged to the Native Americans. European explorers moved through the dark heart of the country at their own risk, never knowing which tribe may have changed its attitude about the whites after being pushed too far. Armed with the most rudimentary of weapons, these individuals were also at the mercy of the weather, wild animals, and even the terrain, where a misstep and broken bone could result in a painful death by dehydration, starvation, or predation.

Around 1618, according to the famous Indian fighter Peter Pence, a Lieutenant Gaston Bushong was accompanying Brulé on his explorations of the New World. Bushong was stationed at a blockhouse in what is now Clinton County. He felt secure and settled in this remote post, and he brought his niece Jacqueline to the blockhouse to live. In time, Bushong would regret his decision.

Apparently, Brulé got out just in time. Restlessness between the French and Indians was at the flashpoint. It may have been because of a trespass, about which the Native Americans were continually sensitive, or an insult by some completely unrelated white man, but for whatever reason, open hostilities broke out between the men at the blockhouse and the Indians.

The blockhouse was attacked, and over the course of the battle, the white men fell one by one. Eventually only six people were left fighting within the walls of the fort: Bushong, Jacqueline, a soldier named LeBrun, and three trappers. And there was only one way to get out of the situation.

During a lull in the fighting, the trappers stealthily loaded a raft at the back of the blockhouse where the Susquehanna River ran past the building. They launched the raft, and the rest of the group made a desperate run for the water. LeBrun was shot in the back, and Bushong and his niece made the mistake of stopping to see if he was still alive. An Indian leaped forward and swung his sword, lopping off Bushong's head. Jacqueline was grabbed and dragged into the bushes, where she too was killed. The trappers managed to escape, but the last hideous image they saw was of a chieftain dancing along the water with Bushong's head before casting it into the stream.

Today Sproul State Forest covers a large portion of Clinton County, and it provides a beautiful setting for a wide range of outdoor activities. But occasionally hikers or fishermen claim to have seen a man rummaging along the water's edge in the misty dusk of a cool summer night, apparently searching for something. Some of the campers have approached, but they suddenly backed off when they saw that the dewy figure, once he stood upright, was missing his head.

The Bones of "Mad Anthony" Wayne

"Mad Anthony" Wayne, in spite of his curious *nom de guerre,* was one of the geniuses of the American Revolution. When the Revolutionary War broke out, he was thirty-one years old and had spent much of his life as a surveyor. He worked the family farm and established a tannery in Chester County. He was elected to the Pennsylvania Legislature and, when the Revolution broke out, had enough influence to raise a regiment of Pennsylvania volunteers. As its colonel, he was wounded at the Battle of Three Rivers in Canada. By February 1777, he was a brigadier general.

He led troops in the Battle of Brandywine and battles at Malvern and Germantown and spent the winter in the encampment at Valley Forge. In 1778, he fought at Monmouth, New Jersey, and in the battle where he received his nickname, Stony Point on the Hudson River.

Seemingly unassailable, Stony Point was a British fort on a 150-foot-high bluff surrounded on three sides by water and on the fourth by a tidal swamp. Cannons studded the walls, and some six hundred redcoats stood at the parapets to ward off any attack. When told of all this by General Washington, Wayne, with supreme confidence in himself, his men, and his commander, replied, "General, if you will only plan it, I will storm Hell!" Overhearing the conversation, a soldier exclaimed, "The man is mad!"

If the soldier had participated in the attack, he would have become convinced his statement was true. To ensure that they surprised the enemy, Wayne ordered his men not to load their weapons, but to rely on their bayonets. During the assault, Wayne was wounded, struck in the forehead by a spent musket ball. Stunned and bleeding, he rose and pressed on, leading his men in the hand-to-hand fighting that ensued. The attack was a success.

He went on to command troops during the fighting and surrender of Cornwallis at Yorktown, Virginia, and then was sent to the fighting in South Carolina and Georgia. As was the case with many military geniuses, however, civilian life was not as kind to Wayne. He lost, as a result of foreclosure, a plantation the state of Georgia had given him in appreciation for his service. He returned to Pennsylvania to serve in the General Assembly. In 1793, his former commander George Washington appointed him as commander-in-chief of the U.S. Army, and Wayne was sent to fight Indians in Ohio.

The British, in violation of the treaty that had ended the Revolution, had never entirely abandoned the Northwest Territory of the Ohio Valley, so the Indians felt confident in attacking settlers flooding the area. In preparation for the upcoming action, Wayne drilled his men diligently. One of the Indian leaders told his warriors, "The Americans are now led by a chief who never sleeps." During the summer of 1794, Mad Anthony Wayne began his advance on the Indians.

In mid-August 1794, his men gazed at an area of land swept by a tornado a few years before. The Indians had used the fallen timber as defensive works in front of the British Fort Miami, and the

desolated area gave the name to the battle that would break the Indian hold on the Northwest Territory: the Battle of Fallen Timbers.

Wayne had studied the Algonquin warriors. He knew that it was their custom not to eat on the morning of a battle. So Mad Anthony sent the Indians word that he was about to attack . . . then delayed for three days. By August 20, the warriors were weak from lack of food and had taken up a battle line instead of fighting as individuals in one-on-one combat as was their usual tactic. The Algonquin line broke before Wayne's well-trained, machinelike infantry. The Indians rushed back to their British allies in Fort Miami, but the British refused to allow them shelter. For this they lost the ability to rely on the Indians for aid in claiming more of America to the west.

The ensuing treaty allowed Wayne to return home to Pennsylvania. He went to Erie in 1796. The years of hard service had taken their toll, and he died at Fort Presque Isle. Yet as famous as he was in American history, one would be at a loss to describe exactly where he is buried.

In 1809, Wayne's family wished to have the General reburied closer to his roots near Philadelphia, so his son Colonel Isaac Wayne went to Fort Presque Isle to fetch the body. Isaac, assuming that after thirteen years in the ground, there wouldn't be much left of the General, sadly underestimated his father's "staying power." He showed up in Erie with just a saddle valise with which to transport what little would be left. When Mad Anthony Wayne's body was exhumed, however, it was virtually intact. What to do?

In what must have seemed like a scene out of a Shakespearean play, Isaac procured a large cauldron, stoked a fire high beneath it, and began to boil the flesh from his father's bones. How long the boiling went on is unrecorded, but the hideous cooking, the bubbling of the water bringing to the surface first a hand, then a foot, then the head and face of his own flesh and blood, must have given Isaac nightmares for decades. Finally the malodorous deed was done. The flesh and clothing were reinterred in Erie at First Street and Ash Street, and Isaac packed the bones in the valise for the journey across the state.

But the valise, it seems, was not packed correctly or secured tightly enough. After several days of riding through the valleys and over the mountains of Pennsylvania, Isaac checked the valise. To his horror, half of his father's bones were gone, strewn along the trail he had ridden through Pennsylvania. Whatever was left in the valise was then buried at St. David's Church in Radnor, Pennsylvania.

Among several explanations for hauntings to occur is the theory that an unconsecrated burial may have an effect on the spirit. Perhaps this is the reason for the sightings, over the years, along the trail strewn with the bones of Mad Anthony Wayne. A mysterious horseman reportedly has been seen, clad in the military uniform of a bygone era. Some, especially in Elk County, think they have identified the rider. He is that great American Revolutionary War hero Mad Anthony Wayne, riding, stopping, searching along the roadside . . . for parts and pieces of his mortal remains.

The Last Frontiersman

Pennsylvania history is filled with tales of frontiersmen, great hunters and trappers. In the early history of this state, it was those daring men who first entered an area. They trapped and hunted and brought back word of the new land and the native people. They often lived peacefully with the natives and seemed to become absorbed by their cultures. In time, some of the Indians and whites intermingled, and many of the mixed-blood descendants likewise earned reputations as great frontiersmen.

Among them was a man named Jim Jacobs. His maternal grandfather was the great Seneca chief Cornplanter, and his father was Captain Jacobs, who founded Fort Kittanning. Jim Jacobs earned a name for himself as a great hunter and trapper. He lived the last years of his life on Cornplanter's reservation. Stories were told of Jacobs's many youthful exploits, but as an old man, he was not happy. Jacobs had wanderlust. He had spent his entire life traveling, living off the land, and taking care of himself. He could not be content to spend his declining years in a village.

For John French of Roulette, Pennsylvania, it was no surprise when he saw old Jacobs one fall morning in 1884 as he walked along through the woods. French had seen the old man many times in the past. He had not seen him for several years, however, and had assumed that old Jacobs had finally given in and settled down to rest for his last remaining years. Yet on this morning, the old man was carrying his flintlock and meandering along as in the past. French stopped to marvel at how well the frontiersman was still getting along.

"Hello!" French called out.

Old Jacobs raised his gun and waved by way of greeting. He stopped and turned back.

"See anything?" asked French.

The old man shook his head. "Too many people. No room for game. It is not as easy to hunt as it used to be." Slight disgust registered in his voice.

"That's the truth," French agreed. "Of course, we're not as young as we once were." Both men laughed.

Then the old man rubbed his whiskers and shook his head. "That's the truth," he said with a sigh.

The two men passed a few more pleasant minutes standing in the woods that cool late-fall day. Eventually their own work called them away, and French smiled as he watched the old hunter fade into the darkness of the trees. The old guy had to be about ninety years old, and still he chose to spend a cold day in the woods hunting. He was amazing.

French did not give another thought to the old hunter until he had cause to go to the Indian reservation a few weeks later. While he was there, he mentioned that he had seen Jim Jacobs recently. French was surprised by the looks he received.

"Jacobs not here anymore," he was informed tersely.

French persisted. Where was old Jacobs living, if not in the village? Surely he was not living alone in the woods somewhere.

One of men he spoke to shook his head. "Much sad," he told the white man. "Three, maybe four winters ago, Jacobs was hit by a train in the night near the town you call Bradford. Next day he was found frozen. Much sad. But still he lived a good life."

French shook his head no. He told the man of his encounter in the woods only weeks earlier.

"Must be spirit of Jacobs," the Indian man replied.

French did not know how to respond. The entire thing must have been a mistake. Someone else must have been killed on those tracks and been mistaken for Jim Jacobs.

A few months later, French had business in Bradford, where the body of the old Indian had supposedly been found. He was there on other business but decided to stop at the newspaper office and check on the story. Inside he met the editor and explained the information that he was looking for. The editor disappeared into a little room and came out with a newspaper. He thumbed through it and pointed to a small article as he laid the paper on the counter.

"Here ya go. Was a bit of excitement about this. An old fella just outside of town knew the Indian well, and he identified him. Some folks were glad to see him go, but others were sorry. The fellow had quite a reputation."

French read down through the article and came across the farmer's name. He knew the man and had no doubt then that it really was Jim Jacobs who was found on the tracks. Jim Jacobs officially died on February 24, 1880, at the age of ninety. But if the story was true, then who had he encountered in the woods? Was the old Indian's spirit wandering along, hunting and enjoying his freedom in death as he had no longer been able to do in life?

The Fiddling Ghost of Ole Bull

Not many people today are aware that Pennsylvania once was fought-over land. The Spanish, Dutch, and French were among the first Europeans to see and covet this land. Long before the British laid claim and drove the Native Americans from their ancestral homes, the French had come and made peace with many of the tribes. In Potter County, a massive block of wilderness was eventually named by the Germans the Black Forest, because the trees grew so thick that sunlight could not penetrate them. Long before the Germans gave the enduring name to this land, however, many other events had scarred it.

In this same county runs what was known historically as the Boon or Boone Road. Its origins are an enigma. When the first American settlers came here in 1808, the road already existed. No one seemed to know who built it or why, but there is little doubt that the road was created in the early or mid-1700s. When early settlers penetrated those woods and found the road, it was already old. They reported deep wagon ruts and young saplings growing up in the middle of the old, abandoned road. Who could have built it?

A legend has lived on in the county that long before the British came to the area, French soldiers were there. As the story goes, a group of French soldiers once tramped through the land. They were armed and had with them a fifer, who played as they marched along. Why they were there, where they were going, and who ordered the march has long been forgotten but history does indicate that there was a French presence in the area in the late 1600s and early 1700s.

According to the legend, this group of French soldiers was ambushed near the head of Kettle Creek by a band of hostile Indians who did not like the encroaching whites. The Frenchmen fought for their lives and won, but in the process, their fifer, who carried only an instrument and not a weapon, was mortally wounded. The Frenchmen could not take along the wounded man and did not have time to tend him where he fell, for they feared that the natives would regroup and return to attack them once more. They quickly made the fifer as comfortable as possible and hurried off, leaving the man little else for comfort but his fife.

For years to come, people have recalled the story of the French fifer and whispered that in the mountains at the head of Kettle Creek, they could hear the fifer still playing his tunes as he marched along. His spirit is said to reside restlessly in the foreign land where he died.

Could it have been this legend that drew world-renowned concert violinist Ole ("OH-lay") Bornemann Bull of Norway to that spot to purchase land more than a hundred years later? Bull's story would become part of the tapestry of the Kettle Creek area. Bull was a young, patriotic Norwegian who could not abide the decision of the Vienna Congress of 1815 to give control of Norway to Sweden. He grew up in an area that seethed with resentment over the loss of Norwegian freedom. In the 1840s, Ole Bull became a violin virtuoso. His talents carried him to the farthest reaches of Europe and eventually to America. Between 1843 and 1845, Bull performed a sold-out concert tour on American soil. Americans seemed to love Ole Bull, and he grew to love America and Americans too.

Bull amassed a fortune while he toured beyond America into Cuba and Canada. During this time, he came up with a plan to recreate Norway in America—a sort of New Norway in the New World. When his tour was over, he returned to the United States in 1852 and began to look for a place that physically reminded him of Norway's steep fjords and valleys. He eventually came to meet a man named John F. Cowan, a land broker in Williamsport, Pennsylvania. Bull described the area he sought, and Cowan insisted that he not only knew of such a spot, but owned the land himself and would be willing to part with it.

Bull was overjoyed. He made the trip to Pennsylvania to see the land and was impressed. The property started at the head of Kettle Creek and ran down a long valley surrounded by high, narrow mountains, reminding Bull greatly of his old homeland. A deal was struck, and Bull bought 11,144 acres of ground. He signed eleven land warrants with Cowan. Ole Bull became an American citizen that October and signed the final deed. The deed included three "reservations" that would be imposed on the new colony. They withheld 658 acres of land in the valley for resale by the former owner at a later date. This was a deadly flaw in Bull's plans, but he did not realize that until much later.

Ole Bull picked a high mountain table and began to build his own home at a place that later would be called Ole Bull Vista. Here he started to construct a feudal castle that would overlook the valley and his envisioned communities. He sent word back to Norway that there was land for sale in four planned Norwegian communities in America. Living conditions were extremely bad in Norway at the time, so many pilgrims were willing to make the journey. Soon Bull's dream began to take shape.

His four planned communities were New Bergan, named for the town where Ole Bull had grown up; Oleanna, named for himself; New Norway; and Walhalla, Americanized into Valhalla and meaning Royal Hall. The communities were soon filled with more than eight hundred people hopeful for a new life and a chance to preserve Norwegian culture and history.

Ole Bull had set for himself and his fledging communities quite a task. Land had to be cleared, fields planted, and a settlement carved out of the wilderness. Unfortunately for Bull and his settlers, the land did not lend itself easily to clearing and cultivating. His people found it terribly hard to clear using their native method of digging up the tree roots rather than simply cutting the trees down. This slowed down their progress considerably. Worse yet was the fact that the ground made very poor cropland. Bull quickly realized that they'd have to initially purchase their foodstuffs from

the town of Coudersport, more than four miles away. During the coming winter, it would be imperative that the road stay open between the Norwegian villages and their supply route, but that would be an arduous task.

Nevertheless, the Norwegians were strong and hopeful. If only they could weather one long winter, they could build up the ground and be more prepared for the following winter. But the following year, a family from Philadelphia named Stewardson informed Ole Bull and the Norwegian immigrants that they were living on borrowed land. It turned out that John F. Cowan had attempted to purchase the ground from the Stewardson family before Ole Bull came to the area. Cowan then had sold the ground to Bull as if he had owned it outright. The deal with Stewardson fell through for lack of funds, and now they wanted their land back. Bull had little choice but to fight the case in court.

He won a judgment against Cowan for the original purchase price of $10,388, but this did not take into account the $25,000 that Bull had invested in the communities or the vast amount of money and labor that the immigrants had invested.

Disheartened and broke, Bull realized he would have to leave his dreamland, which he had once described as "a new Norway, consecrated by liberty, baptized with independence, and protected by the Union's mighty flag." It was said that after the hard struggle, Ole Bull did not see his dream die easily. He stopped construction of his castle and sat amid the ruins, playing the strains of Beethoven on his priceless Stradivarius violin. He stayed in his dreamland as long as possible, wandering the hills around the little towns like a madman and playing frantically.

Eventually Ole Bull came back to his senses and moved on. He had to go back on tour to earn a living again. He married a Frenchwoman, Felicie Villeminot, and had five children. When his first wife died, he married an American woman named Sara Thorp of Madison, Wisconsin, and together they had one daughter.

The immigrants from the Ole Bull communities eventually moved on to Minnesota and Wisconsin, where they settled. Bull did not forget his fellow countrymen and made several trips westward to see them.

In 1872, Ole Bull made his final trip back to Norway, where he settled with his family in the little town of Lysoen. He and Sara visited the United States from time to time, but they never lived there again. Ole Bull died of cancer in 1880, at the age of seventy.

Throughout his life, the pain of his loss in Pennsylvania had haunted him. He had left some of his heart and soul in the Black Forest mountains of Pennsylvania. Had he not been swindled, his dreams would have come true. Though the land was not good for growing produce, it was rich with timber and minerals. Bull had many prominent friends who had been helping his community grow, and through them he had landed a lucrative government contract to build two hundred cannons for the U.S. Army. He had been in the process of purchasing an iron foundry up in Wyoming County to fulfill the contract when he lost his lands.

Today the lands where Ole Bull lived and lost are part of Ole Bull State Park. Little remains of his castle except a sign telling a bit of his tragic tale. However, ever since soon after his death, people have come down from Ole Bull's mountain whispering that they heard phantom music by a violin master played up there. It is believed that upon death, Ole Bull returned to the site of his greatest moment and his greatest loss, and he once more walks his former property playing his violin. The reports are heard most in the fall of the year. Many people believe that in October, Ole Bull visits his home site and plays Beethoven for the world and the woods to hear.

Spirits of Lake Erie

Lake Erie, which borders the Pennsylvania city of Erie, is the site of many ghostly tales. Spirits and phantom ships have been reported on the shore and in the waters.

Since the first white man sailed the Great Lakes, tales of mystery have surrounded the murky waters. Perhaps no tale is more frightening than that of the *Northern Queen,* which eventually earned a reputation as a "death ship." The *Northern Queen* first set sail from Cleveland, Ohio, in 1889. A three-hundred-foot steel ship, she was expected to be good for carrying cargo and netting profits for the owners, but something went terribly wrong. Soon people began to whisper about the evil that seemed to guide the *Northern Queen.* It appeared that the ill-fated vessel had a taste for blood.

A three-masted wooden schooner, the *Fayette Brown,* was sailing on Lake Erie in 1891. The schooner was traveling along without incident, when suddenly the *Northern Queen* came up on her out of nowhere and crashed into her foredeck. The wood yielded easily to the stronger steel. Only one man managed to jump clear of the sinking vessel; the rest of the crew went down with the ship. There was no explanation of how this accident happened.

The *Northern Queen* was a valuable ship, so she was kept in service. On the lakes, things sometimes happen. Fog banks cause ships to strike each other. Human error or other factors also could have come into play.

Fog was given as the official reason why the *Northern Queen* struck another ship from her own fleet named the *North Star* in 1891. This ship went down on Lake Huron. The *Northern Queen* then struck the steamer *G. J. Grammar* near the shores of Lake Huron. The other ship sank to the bottom of the lake.

The *Northern Queen*'s deadly spree was now over. The ship was sunk during a bad storm, but she was raised and put to saltwater usage. She was eventually cut up for scrap in 1925. On the lakes, however, the name of the *Northern Queen* was not soon forgotten. Too many good men had been dispatched into the dark waters for eternity by her steel bow.

The men who worked the ships on the lakes and believed that each had a personality and a life of its own. Some earned reputations as hoodoo ships, where bad things routinely happened. Others were known for having their own way. An example of that would be the U.S. Navy ship the *Michigan,* which was the first iron ship in the Navy. The *Michigan* was supposed to be launched in December 1843 onto the waters of Lake Erie, but she refused for some time to leave the ship building yard. Despite the crew's best efforts, the ship clung stubbornly to the shore. Eventually the yard men left the ship there in disgust. The next morning, the yard crew was surprised to find the *Michigan* floating in the lake offshore all by herself.

The *Michigan* also became famous for the "wishing chair." This chair was given to the captain's steward on a trip to Ontario. A story built up around it that if one sat in it and made a wish, it was certain to be granted. More than one pleased crew member attested that it really worked.

The *Radiant* was a schooner that quietly did the work of her owners for years, until one afternoon after she left Toledo, Ohio, on a normal journey. There were no storms and no reason to suspect that she would not reach her destination, but the schooner simply vanished. Other ships were sent out to look for the missing vessel, but they could find no sign of her. Over the years, people have occasionally claimed to have seen the *Radiant* floating along, but while they watched, the ship suddenly vanished from view.

Not all of Lake Erie's ghosts are on the water. Its islands and shore are said to be haunted by the spirits of those claimed by the lake. Perhaps one of the most notorious of these tales is that of Kelleys Island, where mining once took place.

The island was used to mine limestone during the 1840s. Many ships put in here to load up with the cargo before going back into the danger of Lake Erie. Most of the men mining the limestone on the isle were Italians who seemed gifted at working with the rough rock. One day a mine supervisor ordered the men to blow a new tunnel into another vein of limestone. The men miscalculated, however, and when the explosives blew, the lake burst through and flooded the tunnel filled with men. They had no chance to escape the cold waters of the lake.

After that tragedy, ships began to have difficulty traveling around Kelleys Island. The men said that it was as if someone had ripped the bottoms from their ships. No matter how careful they were, suddenly the ships were in trouble. The sailors began to say that the miners were attacking their ships from the water below. The story of phantom miners tearing holes in the ships lived for many years after the terrible deaths of the miners.

Not all spirits that haunt the lakes are those of sailors or people claimed by the water. Johnson's Island on Lake Erie was pressed into service during the Civil War as a prison camp for Confederate soldiers. It was the perfect place for a prison. The lake surrounded it, so there was nowhere for the prisoners to go. They were at the mercy of the prison guards and the elements. The men were treated shabbily. There were scant supplies, and they often existed on half rations. They suffered terribly from the cold and the winters on the island, with many succumbing to the freezing temperatures that they were not used to. Frostbite, pneumonia, and lung ailments were common causes of death. At one time nearly fifteen thousand Confederate prisoners were on Johnson's island. Those who died there were consigned to cold graves with little sentiment.

After the war ended, the island was no longer used as a prison. The living went home, but the dead were left behind. Today people who have visited the island often tell terrifying stories of feeling watched and a terrible sense of unease. Some report hearing the ghostly sounds of "Dixie" played in the distance and men whispering in Southern accents. The Confederate dead apparently are still trying to live on Johnson's Island.

The Hand from Beyond the Grave

During the industrial revolution, coal was extracted from the ground at a horrific price. Cave-ins and shaft collapses were commonplace. Coal dust explosions ripped men apart as violently as Civil War cannons. More deadly and insidious was the dust that settled in the miners' lungs. Black lung disease robbed men of breath and life long after they had left the mines.

Twelve- and fourteen-hour days were the norm. Company stores charged outrageous prices to miners' families, held captive in the small mining towns by low wages. Mine companies often owned the miners' houses and collected exorbitant rents. The miners could take only so much, and labor disputes grew more common. No disagreement in America was ever as bitter—or deadly—as the rancor between the miners and the mine owners. And no organization was as notorious for violence as the Molly Maguires.

Taking their name from an 1840s Irish movement against unscrupulous landlords, the secret society was reborn in America in 1862. Just days after the Battle of Gettysburg, in July 1863, the Mollies were involved in violent rioting in Philadelphia against the national draft, established to fill the depleting ranks of the Union armies. After the Civil War ended, their goal was to intimidate mine owners, superintendents, bosses, and even police and judges—by strike, threat, and mayhem—into providing higher wages and improved working conditions. Murder in the dead of night was not beyond their scope of operations.

In 1874, the mine owners struck back by hiring Allan Pinkerton, founder of the famed Pinkerton Detective Agency and protector of President Lincoln during the Civil War. His men successfully infiltrated the Mollies. By the next year, they had enough evidence to convict a number of the Molly Maguires on murder charges. With mass executions by hanging in 1877 and 1878, the Mollies were officially disbanded, yet the idea of mine workers banding together in some sort of union was born and would flourish in later years.

The common miners were often caught between the mine officials, who had the law on their side, and the Molly Maguires, whose tactics of intimidation included the delivery of "coffin notices"—notes with a coffin, skull and crossbones, and rosary beads drawn on them—to the target of the Mollies. They often imported violence by bringing Mollies from other parts of the state to commit murder and then disappear. The favor would later be returned. When it came to testifying in court, their stories were all the same and all perjury. For a while, every Molly Maguire had an alibi for every minute during which the heinous acts were committed.

And heinous the crimes were. In 1862, Frank W. J. Langdon was stoned to death. More murders were committed between that year and 1868, all connected to the Molly Maguires. In 1871, mine boss Morgan Powell was murdered.

As if stoning were not savage enough, the murders allegedly committed by the Mollies were particularly cold-blooded. On July 6, 1875, Tamaqua policeman Frank B. Yost was shot in the back while on a ladder extinguishing streetlamps. On September 1 of that year, in the town of Raven Run, Thomas Sanger and his bodyguard, Mr. Uren, left Sanger's home. Sanger was on his way to work at Heaton's Colliery when a Molly Maguire named "Friday" O'Donnell pulled a gun and shot both Sanger and Uren. Sanger, wounded in the arm, ran toward his home. Confronted by another armed Molly, he turned to run but stumbled. A third man, probably Thomas Munley, shot him as he lay on the ground. To ensure that he was dead, a fourth man rolled Sanger over and shot him again. The men ran to a bar, where Munley blurted out to those present, "I shot the first man as he was trying to get into a house." It was a confession that was to seal his fate. In the bar was an undercover agent for the Pinkerton Detective Agency, who would later testify to Munley's statements.

Within two days, another "contract" killing was arranged. John P. Jones had received coffin notices and took to arming himself when he left his house at night. But during the daylight hours, he felt safe. It was a fatal mistake. On September 3, within five minutes of leaving his house for work, he was shot in the back in broad daylight. He managed to run away but staggered and fell into some bushes. Several men followed him and shot him numerous times as he lay defenseless. One of the men was named Jimmy Kerrigan.

Before long, there was a serious legal backlash against the Molly Maguires. A roundup of suspects was made. Trials were set, and Jimmy Kerrigan, in fear for his own life, turned state's evidence and testified, along with the Pinkerton agent, as to the nefarious dealings and premeditated murders of mine bosses and police.

Convictions for murder came by the dozen, and dates were set for the executions by hanging. Six executions were to take place in Pottsville and four more in the Carbon County jail in Mauch Chunk, now known as Jim Thorpe, on June 21, 1877. At least nine more would occur in 1878.

But like many attempts at cracking down, this one may have gone too far. During the panicked sweep of the accused and rush to end the violence, sometimes just being named as a Molly was enough to get someone arrested. And often just being Irish was enough to be named as a Molly Maguire.

Alexander Campbell had emigrated from County Donegal in Ireland in 1868 and settled in Tamaqua, running a tavern there. He moved to the Lansford area in Carbon County, and there he apparently got involved with the Molly Maguires through a fraternal organization, the Ancient Order of Hibernians. But the violent society had not intimidated the sheriff in Carbon County. In a massive sweep, the sheriff arrested ten men for complicity in the murder of Morgan Powell and others. One of those men stood in his jail cell, incredulous at his arrest: It was Alexander Campbell.

Apparently the Mollies had failed to intimidate not only the sheriff of Carbon County, but the judge as well. Ten men were sentenced to hang by the neck until dead. One bragged that he had delivered the Irish vote to Pennsylvania governor Hartranft and waited confidently for his commutation. He was to be horrifyingly disappointed.

Without delving too deeply into the courthouse records, it is difficult to pin down Campbell's exact complicity in the murders of John P. Jones and Morgan Powell. His innocence, however, may perhaps be proven by a message from the other world. Throughout the trial, Campbell maintained his innocence. While incarcerated in cell number 17 in the Jim Thorpe jailhouse, he insisted that he was

not guilty and had been nowhere near where the murders were committed. But mercy was nowhere to be found in the courtroom, and when Campbell heard his fate—to be hanged by the neck until dead—his mood took an otherworldly turn.

June 21, 1877, known for years afterward as the Day of the Rope, had a holiday feel about it—at least for everyone but the ten men sentenced to breathe their last that day. In Pottsville, six men died for the murder of Frank Yost. At 8:30 A.M. in Jim Thorpe, a militia unit called the Easton Grays paraded down the streets to the old prison with loaded muskets, to guard the place of execution from any attempt at freeing the prisoners. The gallows had been set up in the corridor of the building. Shortly after 10:30, the four doomed men left their cells for the last time and, led by Alexander Campbell, walked to the gallows. Each carried a crucifix and was accompanied by a priest. They climbed the thirteen steps and stood over the trap door while hoods were placed over their heads. At 10:48, the trapdoor dropped and the men fell, only to be stopped short by the loop of heavy hemp around their necks.

Two of the men, Donohue and Kelly, struggled at the end of their ropes in a grotesque *danse macabre.* A priest rubbed holy oil on one of the men's hands in an attempt to ease his suffering—which it apparently did not.

Alexander Campbell did not struggle. But he also did not die easily. His was the last heart to stop beating, after a full fourteen minutes—a man holding on to life even after all hope is gone.

And there is other, more bizarre and lasting evidence that Alexander Campbell refuses to die.

Just before he was led off to the gallows, he placed his hand on the icy wall of cell number 17 and murmured, "My mark will stay here as long as the jail stands." He would brand forever, he said, the place where an innocent man was incarcerated before being murdered by the State.

After the mass hangings, the bodies, including that of Alexander Campbell, were taken to their graves. Sometime after that, cell number 17 was occupied by another miscreant. No doubt he called out, frightened and agitated, to the jailer and protested about the strange, clawlike handprint on his wall that he could not rub off. No doubt the jailer, too, tried to erase the mark and failed.

In fact, since 1877, dozens of jailers have painted and repainted the cell wall. In the 1930s, a sheriff named Beigler even had the wall knocked down and replaced. He went to sleep that night satisfied that the spirit of Alexander Campbell had finally been laid to rest. The next morning, he awoke to find that the handprint had reappeared on the new wall. Three decades later, in the 1960s, Sheriff Charles Neast applied a thick coat of green latex paint. But before long, the handprint emerged again.

More recently, James Starrs, a forensic scientist from George Washington University, and Jeff Kercheval, a police chemist from Hagerstown, Maryland, examined the print with infrared photography and other high-tech equipment at their disposal. Their conclusion, according to Starrs, is that "there's no logical explanation for it."

In cell number 17 in the Jim Thorpe jail, Alexander Campbell, from his last day on earth in 1877 to this day, continues to protest his innocence from beyond the grave.

Pittsburgh and Western Pennsylvania

THE PITTSBURGH REGION LONG WAS A LAND IN CONFLICT. THE FRENCH and British fought for control of the land, but eventually the Americans would win it. But even the Americans found Pittsburgh hard to hold. The first test of the constitutionality of the United States came when the people of Western Pennsylvania decided to leave the union to create their own nation. The new country was to be called Westsylvania or Pittsylvania. The region was originally settled by stubbornly independent men and women who were willing to risk everything for freedom beyond all else.

Steel brought a new element of hardness to the western part of the state, and the city of Pittsburgh was birthed in adventure, baptized by blood, and raised with fire and molten steel. Steel was needed to fuel the industrial revolution, and immigrant labor poured into Pittsburgh in the mid-1800s to meet the demand of the nation, which was clamoring for more and more steel. It was a land of wild dreams, where a poor child could grow up to become a rich man. It built breaker boys like little Andy Carnegie into the most powerful men in the world. Along with the wealth came both hard work for the immigrant labor and excesses of wealth.

Western Pennsylvania was also notable as a coal-mining region. As American industrial growth exploded during the Civil War years and for decades thereafter, railroads were built across the continent, and people and goods traveled farther and faster than ever before. Transportation in that era was fueled not by oil, but by anthracite coal, and Western Pennsylvania was one of the main sources.

Today the city continues to influence the world, and the people of the region remain fiercely independent. Though they have faced the loss of the steel mills, Pittsburgh and the rest of Western Pennsylvania still go on.

Joe Magarac, Man of Steel

There was a pride in the immigrant people who worked the steel mills. They grew hard from the work and the heat. The stories of the steel mills were grim, reflecting the reality of life within the burning walls. The heat was unbearable, the men wore scars from bad burns like badges, and the tales of deaths in those buildings were horrifying. The mill workers talked about terrible burns, about men who fell into the crucible of molten steel and simply dissolved in the incredible heat. When the men of Pittsburgh said they poured their very blood into the steel mills, it was sometimes literal. More than one man died that awful death and became part of the steel they produced.

Some mills, like the Jones and Laughlin Steel Works on the south side of Pittsburgh, honored their dead. It is said that one of the ladlemen fell into the liquid steel in Mill Shop #2. That batch was allowed to harden, and the steel was then buried in the yards. Afterward, the men said they saw the ghost of the ladleman moving through the building.

Around the mills, the immigrants began to talk about others who had died. Some told of meeting a man who simply faded away. Others insisted that they saw someone on the girders high up above the liquid steel, who disappeared before their very eyes. But among the spirits that peopled the dangerous world of the steel worker was a man who became a real legend. His name was Joe Magarac, and he was either Hungarian or a Slovak, depending on who told the tale. Was there ever a real Joe Magarac? No one can honestly say. His name denoted his nationality and implied that he was one of those hardworking immigrants. He was supposed to have worked at various steel mills.

Joe was a big man and strong, too. He worked as a ladleman and climbed along the steel girders like a cat while doing his job. As the story goes, one day he slipped and took a terrible fall into the molten steel. It wasn't long after his death that the men began to mutter among themselves that Joe had returned. He was credited with appearing just before several accidents nearly occurred and preventing them. The stories of Joe came home from the mills with the men. They told their wives that a fellow had slipped and nearly plummeted into the liquid steel, only to feel a strong hand grab his leg and haul him back up. When the man was delivered safely to the ground, it was Joe Magarac's face that he saw. Joe smiled and faded away.

Joe was fast becoming a legend to the men of the mills. Over time, his exploits grew from those that were possible to the impossible. No one seemed to care. The men of the steel mills took Joe to heart. In the mills of Pittsburgh, he was bigger than Paul Bunyan, and everyone loved Joe. No one would ever capture the hearts and minds of the steel town like Joe Magarac.

The legend of Joe Magarac dates to before the turn of the twentieth century. Joe was credited with holding together a fifty-ton ladle of liquid steel until the men could flee to safety. He made cannon balls with his bare hands and could commit other great feats of strength.

Joe also had a heart, it seems. According to a tale told by an unnamed worker in the 1930s, Joe fell in love with a blond-haired girl named Mary Mestrovic. Mary was a real beauty, and other men loved her too. Chief among her suitors was a fellow named Pete Prussick.

Her father announced that it was time for Mary to take a husband and said he'd grant her hand to the first man who could lift three dolly bars of steel. He set the contest for the next Saturday, and several men came to try for fair Mary's hand.

Pete Prussick lifted one bar easily and so did another man, but they faltered when the second one was added. A fellow from Johnstown had come to try for Mary, too, and he picked up two bars. The crowd was fearful that the Johnstown man would take away their fair Mary.

Although Pete managed to lift two bars, the third was too much for him. His arms broke, and he was carried away. The Johnstown man also was badly injured. No one could lift the three bars.

Suddenly, from the crowd came a man nearly seven feet tall. He picked up a dolly bar and bent it like a pretzel. The crowd went mad cheering. The man picked up the other two bars and didn't seem to falter at all. Someone called from the crowd for the name of the strong man. The giant turned to them and exclaimed, "I am Joe Magarac!"

The Hungarians and Slovaks roared with laughter. In their native tongue, Magarac meant "jackass." Joe, however, took no offense. He wore his name proudly. He knew they recognized the name and were aware that he was the best steel man ever.

The crowd roared and wanted to give him Mary's hand in marriage. Joe, however, realized that life with him would be hard for the woman he loved, for he was a man of steel. He turned from his love and informed the crowd that he did not have time for marriage. He was born in an ore mine and had come to the Monongahela Valley in an ore car. He lived in the ore pile near the blast furnace and worked all the time. Mary would be better off with a mortal man.

Mary married Pete Prussick, but she always remained Joe's love. Joe knew he could not marry, however, because he was the spirit of the steel mills.

Trotter's Curse

While "Mad Anthony" Wayne may have received his nickname as a backhanded tribute to his reckless courage prior to the Battle at Stoney Point, the cognomen may be closer to the literal truth than the symbolic. A story that comes down to us about the eccentric General is called "Trotter's Curse" and perhaps solidifies the great man's reputation as "mad," not so much in the sense of mental illness, but in the sense of unchecked emotion.

The year was 1792. Wayne was at Pittsburgh, where George Washington had sent him after the Revolution, fighting in the Indian Wars. Like so many brilliant men in history, General Wayne apparently drank alcohol frequently to excess. And like so many people, he evidently was what is called a "mean drunk." It was in one of these murderous, drunken rages that one of his aides, a young man named John Trotter, came to request a favor of his general.

Happenstance placed Trotter before his commanding officer just when the general was at his drunkest and fuming at some personal indignity, real or imagined. Trotter requested a leave to assist his family. Whether Wayne even understood what the young man was asking is unknown. Wayne no doubt cursed, and then replied that he did not care what the man did as long as he left his sight. Trotter, realizing that it was probably not prudent to spend any more time in the presence of Wayne than was necessary, understood this as permission to take his leave, so he left camp to return home to his family.

The alcohol must have been in abundance because, as the story goes, it was several days later when Wayne, now severely hung over, called for Trotter. When told Trotter was not present in camp, Wayne exploded in a furor, cursing the man's name and sending out orders for him to be captured and executed on sight. Three officers were sent out from camp to find Trotter and carry out the disagreeable duty.

Eventually the spirits ran dry and Wayne sobered up. When reminded of his command to have Trotter executed, he immediately rescinded the order. But it was too late. Trotter had been found that morning, read the execution order, and died, no doubt incredulous at the turn of events. Just before he died, predictably, he asked for a Bible. Not so predictably, he began reading Psalm 109. Trotter apparently knew his Bible as well as he knew Wayne. In part, Psalm 109 reads, "Wicked and deceitful mouths are opened against me, speaking against me with lying tongues. They beset me with words of hate, and attack me without cause. . . . So they reward me evil for good, and hatred for my love."

The officers and men must have shuddered at hearing the rest of the psalm: "May his days be few; may another seize his goods. May his children be fatherless, and his wife a widow! May his children wander about and beg . . . and may his memory be cut off from the earth!"

But orders were orders. The three officers knew what would happen to them if they returned to Wayne without having carried out his command. Remembering Wayne's savage temper and vivid, profane vocabulary, to the three officers, Trotter's words must have rung true: "He loved to curse; let curses come on him!"

Could they really be hearing this? Trotter calling down a curse on Wayne? But what Trotter read next must have made their blood run cold: "May this be the reward of my accusers from the Lord, of those who speak evil against my life."

By now the three officers couldn't wait to shut Trotter up. Before another minute passed, Wayne's orders were carried out.

Did the curse stick? One source recounted the lives of the men involved in this miscarriage of justice. One later became a drunk and believed, for the rest of his life, that he was being followed by an invisible mad dog, which many thought was an allegory for Satan himself. One developed diabetes and thirsted continually for the next thirty years. The third apparently went insane, claiming devils possessed him.

And Mad Anthony himself related to friends how, on certain occasions, he would awaken in the middle of the night to see the white, misty wraith of the dead Trotter standing before his cot, his phantom presence accusing Wayne of his drunken miscarriage of justice.

The Phantom Monk

The Benedictine Order of Monks was founded by St. Benedict around the year 529 A.D. Strange as it may seem, some saints appear to have shared many of the characteristics of spirits. St. Benedict, for one, may have had supernatural powers. It has been recorded that he could read the minds of others, made water run from rocks, caused oil to flow continually from a flask long after it should have been empty, and perhaps most miraculously, enabled one of his followers to walk on water.

The Benedictines came to America as an educating presence in 1846, when Saint Vincent Archabbey and College was founded by Boniface Wimmer, a monk from the Benedictine Abbey of Metten in Bavaria. It was the first college in the United States founded under the auspices of the order. On April 18, 1870, the State Legislature of Pennsylvania incorporated the school.

Saint Vincent prides itself on its dedication to Christian ideals and character embodied in the fifteen-hundred-year heritage of the Benedictines. From the beginnings in 1846 of the order's influence in American higher education, Benedictines have gone on to found colleges and schools in six other states. Despite a devastating fire in 1963, the college emerged from the ashes stronger than ever, and it is an influence in Pennsylvania higher education today.

But institutions of higher education often seem to be the settings for strange, otherworldly happenings. And so it is with Saint Vincent. Each year, during the mass accompanying the anniversary celebrations commemorating the founding of the college, one of the robed individuals attending has his hood drawn slightly farther down over his face. Observant students have noticed this monk, who doesn't seem to appear in any of the contemporary records of the college. Of course he doesn't appear in modern records—his photograph was taken in the late nineteenth century. Astute observers recognize him as Boniface Wimmer, the founder of the college, who has been long dead. Perhaps he is checking, as he seemingly does annually, on the welfare of his beloved school.

Haunted by History

Long before the John Heinz Regional History Center was ever built, events happened on its site that were the basis of later ghost stories. The evening of February 9, 1898, started out like every other. People went about their business, and the workers at the Chautauqua Lake Ice Company went about their chores as usual. But at 7:55 P.M., life ceased to be normal for many at the company.

Suddenly the darkness was pierced by blazing fire, and alarms blared out into the night. The ice company building, located in the Strip District between Pike Street and Penn Avenue, was on fire.

Firemen stoically worked at trying to put the fire out. They struggled to get inside the building, where the heart of the blaze flared, but it had iron shutters and was nearly impenetrable. In a desperate move, they climbed to the roof of the building next door and sprayed water on the blaze. There was little else the brave firemen could do.

At 11 P.M., the building suddenly exploded. Flames shot up more than a hundred feet into the sky. The roof burst open, and steel pipes, girders, and stones from the walls rained down for several blocks. People ran for their lives. Many firemen, onlookers, and neighbors were struck and killed by the debris, and dozens more were badly injured.

The owner of the building, William Scott, stood watching his world go up in flames. He shouted at the firemen that men were inside the building. He tried to help, but there was little that he could do. He had no idea that he was about to lose so much more than his livelihood. When the building finally blew up, two of his sons were killed in the blast.

By dawn, the entire city of Pittsburgh was abuzz about the tragedy. In the end, eighteen people had died, and many more were injured. The building had been destroyed, and the company was gone.

The building remained in ruins for some time, but eventually it was rebuilt and put to other uses. Today it is the John Heinz Pittsburgh Regional History Center. Since shortly after the building opened, the staff have had ghostly tales to tell. Though there are many historical objects throughout the building, the ghosts do not seem to be associated with them. Instead, they seem to date from that terrible fire.

On the fifth floor, the center has a storage area and historical archive. That is said to be the most spiritually active area of the building. Security guards have seen a male figure moving on that floor, but wandering the halls and through the archive, he does not trip the motion sensor alarms. The security staff has also reported seeing a figure on the loading docks who disappears when approached. The phantom is wearing clothing from the turn of the twentieth century.

Staff members have seen specters speaking to some of the exhibits. The spirits don't seem to realize that these are electronic exhibits and not human beings. Perhaps that is because when their mortal bodies passed on in 1898, such things did not exist. Staffers have also reported phantom footsteps, doors opening and closing on their own, objects moving, and disembodied voices.

People seem more intrigued than frightened by the spirits in the building, who seem to be curious about what has happened to the old Chautauqua Lake Ice Company. Perhaps they are enjoying the stroll into the past that the center provides them.

The Lost Town of Livermore

In its heyday, Livermore in Westmoreland County was quite a nice little town. It was incorporated into a borough in 1863. It had thriving businesses and a little school, and forty-plus families lived in Livermore at that time. The town was named for Alonzo Livermore, an engineer for the old Pennsylvania Canal system. It was aptly named, because the town derived its economy from the canal system. But as the fortune of the canals declined, the reason for the locks did too. Soon the railroad carried mail, goods, and travelers to the little town.

The death knell rang for Livermore in part because of the St. Patrick's Day flood of 1936, which swept away fourteen homes. Residents had to take refuge that long night high in the hills that surrounded the town. When they returned to see what they could rebuild after the flood, they were told not to bother. It was announced that the town had been pronounced dead by the state government.

In 1950, Livermore was flooded as part of the Conemaugh River Lake Flood Control Project. Citizens were very concerned about the proposed flooding of their town. People in Livermore wanted to know what would happen to them. Where were they supposed to go? Their homes would be gone, their churches and school destroyed. The generations of dead in their cemeteries would be in jeopardy. Their entire way of life was being destroyed, along with their memories.

Unfortunately for the folks of Livermore, the government stops for no man or community. People could be moved. Churches and schools could be found elsewhere. Memories have no commercial value. And the dead could be dug up and moved to another spot. They could not complain.

This was exactly the fate that befell the entire town. People were bought out and left. Some were grateful for the new start; others wept at the loss of a generations-old family homestead. Folks found new homes, churches, and schools in other towns, but for the dead, it was different. The town didn't want to scatter the dead among the many cemeteries in the area. Family plots would have to be moved, and then there were the graves of the dead who had no living relatives to speak for them. In the end, a few families moved their dead to other cemeteries, but the majority of folks decided to leave their deceased loved ones in the newly created Livermore Cemetery above the floodplain.

The feelings of many who grew up in Livermore were recorded by Peggy and Ruthie Oliver, who wrote in *History of Livermore: A Canal Town,* "It has been said 'Our soil belongs also to the unborn generations.' How sad this did not hold true for Livermore, because the friendly little community became a legend in 1950 to make way for the Conemaugh Dam."

The entire town was subsequently flooded, and stories began to surface that Livermore was haunted. Folks claimed that since the town was vacated and then flooded without the destruction of the buildings, the dead still haunted the town.

Most of the paranormal tales have centered around the graves disturbed when the cemetery was moved to higher ground before the town was flooded. Sightings have been reported of people moving through the cemetery as if wandering about looking for something. If approached, the phantoms simply disappeared. Locals believe that these are the dead looking for their original graves. Apparently the dead of Livermore have been able to show their dissatisfaction with their fate. People have reported hearing phantom church bells still ringing on Sunday mornings. Some visitors have insisted they saw people walking on the water—specters who seemed to be searching for something beneath the dark waters of the dam. Perhaps these spirits are looking for their homes and final resting places. Others have sighted ghostly buildings above the water under which they now reside.

George Romero filmed part of his original *Night of the Living Dead* movie in Livermore Cemetery. The eerie scene where Johnny and his sister Barbara go to visit their dead father was shot there. The tone of the movie was set by the moment when Johnny tells his sister, "They're coming to get you, Barbara." There is a terrible feeling that people are watching you from behind the headstones and just might be "coming to get you" while you're in that cemetery.

Perhaps the most disconcerting stories have come from those who reported feeling as if they were being intensely watched or even followed. People have heard footsteps walking behind them. Some even claim that a black shadow has been seen following folks visiting the cemetery, and that this spirit has pushed people down. There is more than one account of someone being shoved or forced to the ground while no one is near him or her. Stories are also told of people feeling as if something reached out to grab their legs while they were walking through the cemetery.

It seems that the spirits of the dead town and its dead residents linger there hauntingly to let people know that all is not well in the village these days. No indeed, all is not well, and perhaps the dead of Livermore are still waiting for their town to be resurrected.

The Strange Disappearance of Oliver Lerch

It was December 24, 1890, in Indiana County. Mrs. Lerch looked around the living room of the large farmhouse that she shared with her husband and grown children and smiled. The light from the kerosene lamps cast a soft glow across the buffet table, which was laden heavily with food for the Christmas Eve celebration. It had snowed hard earlier that day, and she had feared that the party would have to be canceled. But early in the afternoon, the snow had finished laying down a new layer, and people had come out for the evening's festivities after all. Mrs. Lerch brushed past her husband with a smile and gave him a pat on the arm. He was talking with two of their neighbors and the Reverend about a new church roof that was being planned for the spring.

She stopped to speak to guests here and there in the parlour and the good front room. There must have been at least twenty folks at the party, and they were all enjoying themselves immensely. Mrs. Lerch was glowing with the compliments that came her way over the food. A roasted venison joint sat side by side with a large, plump turkey that she had roasted in the cookstove since the wee hours of the morning. These were accompanied by potatoes, yams, pumpkin pies, and a dazzling display of cakes and cookies. Jam pots and a crock of freshly churned butter kept their posts near a mountain of just-baked breads and biscuits. It had nearly worn Mrs. Lerch out to prepare the feast, but it had been worth it.

In the kitchen, she found her daughter puttering with the large coffee percolator. "I think we'd better get another pot of coffee on," she said. "This one's near finished." Mrs. Lerch bustled forward and shook the pot on the stove. Sure enough, it was about two-thirds empty. She pushed back the pot simmering on the stovetop and lifted the cookstove lid to poke at the fire within. She shoved a couple small sticks of wood into the stove to create a bit more heat.

"Fill that coffeepot and bring it over here," she instructed her daughter. The girl filled the pot from a bucket of cold water sitting on the dry sink. "This will just about finish the bucket," the girl said.

"Don't worry, I'll send Oliver for more," her mother replied.

Mrs. Lerch poked at the fire to stir it back to life. It crackled greedily around the sticks of wood. Satisfied, she clapped the lid back down over the firebox and set about filling the coffee grinder with beans. After she ground them, she put them in the percolator and set the pot on to cook. Wiping her hands on a towel, Mrs. Lerch picked up the two buckets on the dry sink and set them on the table. She'd send Oliver to the pump in the front yard for more water before it slipped her mind.

In the parlour, Mrs. Lerch found her son poking at the fire in the fireplace. He had just come in from filling the woodbox and was tending the fire.

"Oh good, Oliver," Mrs. Lerch said by way of greeting. "You're already bundled up. Would you take the water buckets out to the pump and fill them for me?"

The tall, handsome twenty-year-old smiled down at his plump, little mother. "Sure, Ma. I'll get the water in just a second. I've got to build up the fire a bit. There's no wind out there, but it sure is cold."

Mrs. Lerch nodded, patted her son on the back, and moved off to say a few words to one of the ladies whom she hoped would be helping with the church rummage sale in a few weeks.

Absently, Mrs. Lerch saw Oliver go to the kitchen and heard the familiar clank of the buckets. The kitchen door opened and closed. Oliver knew how she hated him tracking up the floor, and he was using the kitchen door so as to make less mess.

Mrs. Lerch turned back to her conversation, but it was suddenly interrupted by screams from outside. It was Oliver, and he was screaming something. The whole house fell silent for a second, in shock. Then, as a group, everyone ran for the door. Mrs. Lerch led the way, moving faster than her plump, little legs looked capable of carrying her. The assemblage plunged out into the frigid darkness and around the side of the porch to where the pump stood. Light beamed out of the windows, and that along with strong moonlight afforded them a very good view.

They were startled to see Oliver floating off the ground and upward. He had dropped one of the pails as he thrashed and twisted, trying to fight off an invisible force that seemed to be lifting him skyward. "Help, it's got me!" the young man cried out in panic over and over again as he drifted ever upward.

The family and friends watched in horror as Oliver quickly floated up into the darkness. His panic-filled voice reached them from the darkness for a brief time after he was gone from view, but not one among them knew how to help the young man. Who had him? He had screamed that something had him, but no one saw or heard anything other than the panicked young man. Who or what had grabbed him up and carried him off?

A group of men walked toward the pump. The minister was among them, and he held out his arm to stop them. "Wait, we should look for tracks. In this snow, there should be tracks."

The men turned their eyes toward the snow. One empty bucket lay a few feet from the pump, and a set of tracks made its way from the kitchen door to the spot where the bucket lay. Beyond that point, all was smooth, white snow. No other tracks were found in or around that area.

Oliver Lerch seemed to have ceased to exist. He never returned home, and his family never learned of his fate. For the rest of her life, Mrs. Lerch would be tormented by horrible visions of what had taken her boy. Demons? Creatures from another world? No explanation gave her any relief. So what did grab up Oliver and carry him off? No one has answered that riddle to this day.

Bibliography

Books and Journal Articles

Asfar, Dan. *Ghost Stories of Pennsylvania.* Edmonton, Alberta: Ghost House Books, 2002.

Baughman, Jon. *Strange and Amazing Stories of Raystown Country.* Roaring Spring, PA: Pine Creek Press, 1987.

Brua, Charles. "A Ghost Story." *Penn State Magazine* (Sept.–Oct. 1998).

Chamberlain, Joshua Lawrence. *The Passing of the Armies.* Dayton: Morningside Bookshop, 1982.

Flannery, Mark C. "Wiestling Hall." n.p., 1969.

Hauck, Dennis William. *Haunted Places.* New York: Penguin Books, 1996.

Jorgenson, Jay. *The Wheatfield at Gettysburg: A Walking Tour.* Gettysburg, PA: Thomas Publications, 2002.

Lyman, Robert R. Sr. *Ole Bull: Forbidden Land . . . Strange Events in the Black Forest.* Coudersport, PA, 1971.

Nesbitt, Mark. *The Ghost Hunter's Field Guide: Gettysburg and Beyond.* Gettysburg, PA: Second Chance Publications, 2005.

———. *Ghosts of Gettysburg: Spirits, Apparitions and Haunted Places of the Battlefield.* Gettysburg, PA: Thomas Publications, 1991.

———. *Ghosts of Gettysburg III: Spirits, Apparitions and Haunted Places of the Battlefield.* Gettysburg, PA: Thomas Publications, 1995.

———. *Ghosts of Gettysburg IV: Spirits, Apparitions and Haunted Places of the Battlefield.* Gettysburg, PA: Thomas Publications, 1998.

———. *Ghosts of Gettysburg V: Spirits, Apparitions and Haunted Places of the Battlefield.* Gettysburg, PA: Thomas Publications, 2000.

———. *Ghosts of Gettysburg VI: Spirits, Apparitions and Haunted Places of the Battlefield.* Gettysburg, PA: Second Chance Publications, 2004.

———. *More Ghosts of Gettysburg: Spirits, Apparitions and Haunted Places of the Battlefield.* Gettysburg, PA: Thomas Publications, 1992.

Oliver, Peggy, and Ruthie Oliver. *History of Livermore: A Canal Town.*

Pfanz, Harry W. *Gettysburg: The Second Day.* Chapel Hill: University of North Carolina Press, 1987.

Robtham, Rosemarie. "America's Ten Most Haunted Houses." *Life* (Nov. 1980).

Stone, David, and David Frew. *The Lake Erie Quadrangle: Waters of Repose.* Erie, PA: Erie County Historical Society.

Stonehouse, Frederick. *Haunted Lakes II.* Coudersport, PA: Leader Publishing Company, 2000.

Swetnam, George. *Pittsylvania Country.* New York: Duell, Sloan, and Pearce, 1951.

Thomas, Elizabeth H. *A History of the Pennsylvania State Forest School, 1903–1929.* Mont Alto, PA: State Forest Academy Founders Society, 1985.

Tucker, Glenn. *High Tide at Gettysburg: The Campaign in Pennsylvania.* New York: Bobbs-Merrill Company, 1958.

Wilson, Patty A. *Haunted Pennsylvania.* Laceyville, PA: Belfry Books, 1998.

———. *The Pennsylvania Ghost Guide.* Vol. 1. Roaring Spring, PA: Piney Creek Press, 2000.

———. *The Pennsylvania Ghost Guide.* Vol. 2. Roaring Spring, PA: Piney Creek Press, 2001.

Wilson, Patty A., and Scott Crownover. *Boos and Brews: A Guide to Haunted Taverns, Inns and Hotels of Pennsylvania.* Roaring Spring, PA: Piney Creek Press, 2002.

Websites

www.aolsvc.worldbook.aol.com/wb/Article?id=ar079760. "Brulé, Etienne."

www.carbonecon.com/activities/history.htm

www.delcoghosts.com/carbon_co_jail.html

www.forgottenoh.com/Counties/Champaign/lincoln.html

www.geocities.com/ri_aoh/mollies/htm

www.lehigh.edu/-ineng/paw/paw-history.htm

www.members.aol.com/spiritNRGs/PJTjail.html

www.paranormal-insight.com/carbonjail.html

www.placeswelike.com/ireland

www.rootsweb.com

Newspaper Articles

"Auras of History, Supernatural Permeate Baker Mansion," *Tribune-Democrat,* March 1981.

"Haunted Hall Homeplace for Headless Horseman," [State College] *Centre Daily Times,* August 8, 1969.

"A Haunting Picture," [Hagerstown, MD] *Herald Mail,* October 31, 2003.

"History of Livermore—A Canal Town," by Peggy and Ruthie Oliver.

"Life Staffers H(a)unt for Ghost at Mansion," *Altoona Mirror,* September 1980.

"Livermore Girls," *Little Monitor,* October 1871.

"The Mont Alto Ghost," *Allegheny News,* Summer 1995.

"Reed Had Threatened to Kill Hurley Girl," *Chambersburg Public Opinion,* May 11, 1911.

"Spectral Specters Frequent Mont Alto Campus," [University Park] *PA Daily Collegian,* October 1994.

"What Goes Bump in the Night at Penn State Mont Alto?" *Record Herald,* October 1994.

Acknowledgments

We would like to acknowledge our editor, Kyle Weaver, and his assistant, Amy Cooper, as well as artist Heather Adel Wiggins, copyeditor Joyce Bond, and designer Beth Oberholtzer. Mark thanks his wife, Carol, for her constant support and eternal patience. Patty thanks Scott and the children for their encouragement and love.

About the Authors

Mark Nesbitt is the author of *Ghosts* *of Gettysburg,* a six-volume series that received the National Paranormal Award in 2004. Formerly a National Park Service ranger and then a battlefield guide, he has lived in Gettysburg since 1971. He has also written several Civil War history titles, including *Through Blood and Fire, Saber and Scapegoat,* and *35 Days to Gettysburg.*

Patty A. Wilson writes about the para-normal and Pennsylvania folklore and is the author of *The Pennsylvania Ghost Guide, Where Dead Men Walk,* and *Boos and Brews.* She lives with her family in central Pennsylvania, where she has pursued her writing for thirty years. Her articles have appeared in several publications, including *FATE Magazine* and *Countryside.*

Other Titles in the

Haunted Series

HAUNTED NEW JERSEY
by Patricia A. Martinelli and Charles A. Stansfield, Jr.
978-0-8117-3156-0

HAUNTED NEW YORK
by Cheri Revai • 978-0-8117-3249-9

HAUNTED OHIO
by Charles A. Stansfield, Jr. • 978-0-8117-3472-1

HAUNTED WEST VIRGINIA
by Patty A. Wilson • 978-0-8117-3400-4

Other Titles in the

Haunted Series

HAUNTED CONNECTICUT
by Cheri Revai • 978-0-8117-3296-3

HAUNTED DELAWARE
by Patricia A. Martinelli • 978-0-8117-3297-0

HAUNTED FLORIDA
by Cynthia Thuman and Catherine Lower
978-0-8117-3498-1

HAUNTED GEORGIA
by Alan Brown • 978-0-8117-3443-1

HAUNTED ILLINOIS
by Troy Taylor • 978-0-8117-3499-8

HAUNTED JERSEY SHORE
by Charles A. Stansfield, Jr.
978-0-8117-3156-0

HAUNTED MAINE
by Charles A. Stansfield, Jr.
978-0-8117-3267-3

HAUNTED MARYLAND
by Ed Okonowicz • 978-0-8117-3409-7

HAUNTED MASSACHUSETTS
by Cheri Revai • 978-0-8117-3221-5

HAUNTED
NEW YORK CITY
by Cheri Revai • 978-0-8117-3471-4

HAUNTED TEXAS
by Alan Brown • 978-0-8117-3500-1

HAUNTED VERMONT
by Charles A. Stansfield, Jr.
978-0-8117-3399-1

WWW.STACKPOLEBOOKS.COM • 1-800-732-3669